BE THE
BIGGER PERSON

BE THE
BIGGER PERSON

SCENARIOS & SOLUTIONS TO **BETTER YOURSELF**

AVNI PAREKH

For more information about bulk purchases, please contact Avni Parekh at Support@BTBPbook.com or visit www.BTBPbook.com or www.BeTheBiggerPersonBook.com and fill out the contact form.

Author headshot by Monica Scardina

Printed in the United States of America

Print ISBN: 978-0-9995064-0-0
eBook ISBN: 978-0-9995064-1-7

"I count him braver who overcomes his desires than him who conquers his enemies; for the hardest victory is over self."
—Aristotle

This book is dedicated to you—the reader.
In it contains the gift of harnessing a new perspective.
May you be inspired to create your destiny and find the strength
to pursue your dreams, despite the obstacles you may encounter
and the challenging moments you will face in your lifetime.

CONTENTS

- You pet-sat for a friend and the pet destroyed your home
- Your best friend and partner do not get along
- A friend talks negatively about everyone and everything in his or her life
- A friend stole from you
- A friend asks you for a lot more than you get in return
- You feel left out of group activities with friends
- A friend keeps canceling plans
- A friend is dating or involved with your ex-partner

- You were dumped
- You and your partner got into an argument and are not speaking to each other
- You are not getting enough attention in your relationship
- Your partner is emotionally unavailable
- You are cheating on your partner
- You love your partner but still think about your ex-partner
- Your partner is abusive
- Your partner has a wandering eye or acts overly flirtatious
- You contracted a sexually transmitted infection (STI)
- Your partner misled you about the seriousness of your relationship
- You do not trust your partner anymore
- Your partner is cheating on you
- Your spouse wants a divorce
- Your long-distance relationship is not working out
- You are not in love with your partner anymore

- Your property sustained damage and requires costly repairs
- Your neighbor is not considerate of others
- Neighborhood kids vandalized your property
- Your house was destroyed by someone you entrusted its care to
- A car is parked in your assigned parking space
- You cannot afford to pay your rent or are being evicted or foreclosed on

- Your house has a pest infestation
- Your tenants are a nightmare to deal with
- Your roommate unexpectedly moved out
- You have been displaced from your home
- Your landlord is not helpful and/or rude
- You are having difficulty selling your house
- A neighbor's party is getting loud and rowdy
- Your house was robbed
- You are ashamed of your house and do not bring anyone over

- You feel like your boss is making your work-life difficult
- You think a coworker is trying to undermine your hard work
- You were fired or laid off
- Your workload is increasing and it is hindering your productivity
- You think you deserve a promotion, raise or title-change
- You were referred to do business with a coworker's
  relative or friend and got ripped off
- You trusted a coworker with a secret and they told
- You were written up
- You were demoted
- You feel you were short-changed on your severance package
- You do not like your coworkers
- You did not receive a bonus
- An employee is not meeting your expectations
- You are being harassed by a coworker
- You are unemployed and cannot find a job

- Your grades are below average
- You feel like you may not get accepted into a university
- There is a rumor being spread about you
- Your SAT and/or ACT scores were not as high as you
  expected
- You were suspended or expelled
- You are worried because you found out you are pregnant

- You think a friend may need serious emotional help
- You are being teased because of your religion or ethnicity
- You are being teased because of how you look
- You are being teased because of your sexual orientation
- You are being bullied online and/or in person
- You are being peer-pressured to do something you would not ordinarily do
- You failed a class
- You cannot financially keep up with your friends
- You want to commit suicide

- A driver cut you off
- A driver stuck their middle finger at you
- You are being tailgated or angrily honked at by a driver exhibiting road-rage
- A driver is weaving in and out of traffic
- A driver is texting
- A driver next to you is blasting their music
- You were pulled over for speeding and/or drag-racing
- A motorcyclist is driving erratically
- Your car got towed
- A bicyclist is blocking your lane
- You are stuck in a traffic jam
- You got into an accident
- You received a traffic ticket
- Your car broke down on the road
- You were indicating for a parking space and another driver took it

- A flight attendant is being rude
- The passenger seated next to you is being rude
- The passenger seated next to you will not stop talking to you
- A passenger is snoring loudly
- A passenger's baby will not stop crying

- A passenger is playing their music or movie loudly
- Your flight was delayed or got diverted
- You missed your flight
- Your carry-on luggage needs to be checked
- Your luggage and/or belongings were lost or stolen
- A passenger is rushing to disembark the plane
- The passenger sitting next to you smells bad
- You were kicked off the flight for unruly behavior
- The passenger seated in front of you keeps pushing their seat back
- You were sexually harassed or groped by a passenger on the plane

CHAPTER 9: TRAGEDY
- A loved one died unexpectedly
- You are involved in a lengthy and/or messy legal battle
- You were raped or molested
- A loved one was paralyzed
- You survived a horrific, life-changing event
- You or a loved one were diagnosed with a terminal condition
- A loved one committed suicide
- A loved one is suffering from a mentally or physically debilitating disease
- You were pregnant and had a miscarriage
- You caused an accident where a person or many people died
- You were a victim of police brutality
- You or a loved one is addicted to drugs and/or alcohol
- You are taking care of a chronically ill parent, spouse or child
- You think you have ruined your life
- You or a loved one suffer from obesity

CHAPTER 10: PUBLIC PLACES
- You are receiving poor service
- A stranger is being rude to you for no reason
- You got into a heated argument or fight with a stranger
- Someone is invading your personal space
- There is no accommodation for your disability
- You are being harassed or hollered at by disrespectful men

- Someone's child is being obnoxious or is out of control
- Someone is smoking cigarettes near you
- A woman is breastfeeding
- A friend is acting drunk and disorderly
- Your patience is wearing thin
- A couple is displaying excessive affection for each other
- You got drunk and feel like you made a fool of yourself
- You feel you were discriminated against
- You got arrested

ACKNOWLEDGEMENTS

Infinite gratitude goes to God, the almighty creator behind it all. I couldn't have brought this book into the world without His guidance, support and love.

An abundance of gratitude goes to my mother, Kalpana Mistry—a refugee of the Idi Amin dictatorship in Uganda, and a single mother of two who diligently worked her way to the top—for giving me the gift of life and for always demonstrating humility.

Immense appreciation goes to Kalpana Mistry and Therese Costa for acting as my editors and to Claudia Quintana for proofreading.

Writing this book has been a journey and I'm grateful for every experience and every person that has shaped my thinking.

INTRODUCTION

Dear Reader,

Do you want to be happy in life? If the answer is "yes," then you've come across the right book.

Life-satisfaction is defined as the level of contentment a person feels within all aspects of their life. Let's be real, it can be difficult to be satisfied with life when it's full of ups and downs. In fact, it's tough enough just to survive and make a living.

Sometimes, the most mundane and petty situations we experience can rub us the wrong way and have a lasting effect on our psyche and overall well-being, which can hinder us from moving forward with daily plans, yearly goals and even life itself. As a matter of fact, it has been widely documented that when we foster negative emotions like anger and frustration, our heart rate goes up, our blood pressure increases and our stomach produces more acid causing heartburn, indigestion and other health problems. Overall, these emotions are very damaging to our body, mind and spirit. However, by maintaining a positive state of mind, we all have the ability to remain in good physical health while overcoming the challenges we face, especially on a day-to-day basis.

Be The Bigger Person: Scenarios & Solutions to Better Yourself is unlike any other book on the market because it incorporates several aspects of our public and private lives—family, friends, relationships, academia, work, driving, flying, tragedies and even public places—into a simple, easy-to-read guide that can benefit the entire family.

The tips and solutions you're about to read have a proven effect to improve your mood, reduce your stress, and help you lead a more satisfying and fulfilling life.

In this book, I present readers with a simple, three-tier process to help them overcome the situation they are dealing with. In order to make use of this book, refer to the table of contents and find the situations relevant to you. Once you flip to the corresponding page, you'll first be presented with the situation or "scenario" in question. Second, two brief, main points are outlined that provide you with an honest view of the situation. Third, since everything that happens in life is about perspective, a positive takeaway or "solution" is suggested. By the time you reach the end of the book, you will have gained insight into a variety of life experiences, whether you have personally experienced them or not.

The goal of the three-tier process is to offer short, practical tips, answers and suggestions about the situation at hand and the intention of the solution is to help the reader recondition their mind and create a new perspective about the situation, their day, their life or even their own self-image. And if more information is needed about how to cope with the issues readers may be facing, then a multitude of resources are provided to help promote positive outcomes.

In my own life, I have experienced a plethora of situations—beginning with my parents' bitter and tumultuous divorce to other distressing childhood experiences, coupled with several traumatic issues faced in adulthood—that could have caused my outlook on life to shift in a negative direction. Personally, the positive and especially the negative experiences I've had in my life have helped me gain a better understanding about human nature, the need for people to work together in harmony, and what I can do as a human being to better myself and the world we live in. Ultimately, my cumulative life experiences have taught me that the power of harnessing a new perspective is tremendous, in fact, it can change your life—as it has certainly helped mine.

Since childhood, I always had an innate curiosity about life and our purpose on this earth. The inspiration for writing this book comes from my own life experiences, situations I have guided friends through, and other pressing issues I have seen on TV or read in the news. I decided to write this book because it became evident to me that there weren't any resources in one place that focused on guiding people through common stressful situations.

I know that every one of us can contribute to reducing conflict by being more mindful of how we treat others and by choosing to take the higher road when faced with difficult situations. Give yourself the gift of gaining a new perspective and let go of negative thoughts that can lead you in a repetitive cycle that only travels in one direction: downhill.

When we change our perspective—by trying to extract the positive lesson in every situation—we develop a better outlook on life and the experiences we go through. Therefore, we should all make an active effort to better ourselves, and I encourage all readers to "be the bigger person."

Change your perspective, change your life—it's that simple.

Are you up for the challenge?

Sincerely,

Avni Parekh

#BTBP CAMPAIGN

"BTBP stands for 'be the bigger person.' It is a motto used to help remind people to choose the higher road in life, rather than succumb to anger when faced with negative situations."
–Avni Parekh

There is nothing better than the feeling of paying it forward.

Help your family and friends rise above the negative experiences they encounter on a day-to-day basis by using the hashtag #BTBP when engaging them and others on social media. It could make all the difference in brightening someone else's day.

For more inspiration, log onto www.BTBPbook.com or visit:

- Facebook: @BTBPbook
- Twitter: @BTBPbook
- Instagram: @BTBPbook

To connect with Avni, log onto www.AvniParekh.com or visit:

- Facebook: @Avni.USA
- Twitter: @AvniParekh
- Instagram: @AvniParekh

CHAPTER 1

FAMILY

*"The key is to keep company only with people
who uplift you, whose presence calls forth your best."*
–**Epictetus**

E very person is born into a family and each family is different. Part of what is so special about families is that they are made up of many people, all with personalities of their own. Sometimes these personalities mesh well together and other times they don't. Regardless of each different personality type, one factor is certain, all people—young or old—have an innate need to feel accepted, and this need for acceptance or a sense of belonging is more powerful within your own family unit than anywhere else.

As a matter of fact, the need for acceptance begins as soon as a person is born. Meaning, it is important to cultivate a healthy relationship and dialogue with every member of the family, including children. Children are very perceptive and though they may not have much life experience under their belt, they possess a sense far more powerful than experience, called intuition. The greatest gift parents can give their children is emotional security, and this is achieved by offering a listening ear—free of judgment— and an advocating voice to support them when they need help.

A person's family should serve as their support system, and every member of the unit needs consistency and stability regardless of their age. There are many wonderful memories family members cherish with one another and there are also many aggravating moments experienced within family life that can cause stress and emotional pain. For instance, what if your child is rebelling or your relationship with your sibling has gone downhill? How you handle these situations and other challenging moments you experience in life has a direct correlation to your success and overall happiness.

Foremost, no family that exists on this planet is perfect, even if it may appear as such. In fact, everyone has to face the reality that life is not perfect and the people we care about are not perfect either. Secondly, every member of the family has a role and responsibility to make the dynamic work, starting with the parent. The family unit should be full of guiding forces that are willing to help one another through the ups and downs of life.

If you care about the people in your life, especially your family, it is worthwhile to try and resolve your problems together. When trying to resolve issues amicably, it is important to have sincere and meaningful dialogue that reinforces each family member's need for acceptance and self-respect, while providing encouragement that the hurdle can be overcome, thereby restoring a member's sense of emotional security within that family unit. If, during this process, you realize that there will not be a resolution you can agree upon, then at least you know you tried. Trying is half the battle, knowing is the other half.

A family member deceived you. Consider the following,

A) Make sure you have all the facts.

B) When people show you their true colors, take it for what it is worth.

Takeaway: In life, it is wise to be sure you have all the facts before jumping to any conclusions. When a family member purposely or maliciously deceives you, it is important to keep in mind, not everyone may have your best interest at heart and sometimes that includes family members. As unfortunate as that may be, it is better to know a person's intentions toward you as opposed to not knowing. So, when people show you their true colors, take it for what it is worth. Someone else's poor behavior is a reflection of them, not you.

You think your parents are too strict. Consider the following,

A) Parents have more life experience under their belt and, in most cases, have your best interest at heart.

B) Parents have a responsibility to make sure their children are safe.

Takeaway: Like it or not, parents are responsible for their children, including teaching them right from wrong and setting limitations to what they can and cannot do. Part of this responsibility is to make sure their children are safe, and sometimes it can come off as being overbearing. Instead, look at it from this perspective, with age comes the ability to predict how certain situations can turn out, and when you think your parents are being too tough on you, it is not because they do not want you to have fun, it is because their life experience has taught them that some situations can be dangerous or lead to an unfavorable outcome. Loving parents have their children's best interest at heart and want to help them keep out of trouble and stay safe.

You are being abused by your caretaker(s). Consider the following,

A) No one has the right to physically, verbally, emotionally and/or sexually abuse you.

B) Get help immediately.

Takeaway: When the person or people caring for you are abusing you, it is not an easy situation to be in. Caretakers have a responsibility to nurture the people in their care, this includes children as well as adults. If loving-care is being replaced with physical, verbal, emotional or sexual abuse, you owe it to yourself to get help. There are people out there who have a genuine interest in your well-being who you can confide in, for instance, teachers, policemen, firemen, friends and even family members who may not be aware of your situation, are all good options to consider.

Your parent(s) abandoned you. Consider the following,

A) Some people are not wired to be nurturing parents.

B) You are not a victim nor are you unwanted.

Takeaway: The experiences people have throughout their lifetime can have a profound effect on their psyche, alter their perceptions about life, and can interfere with how they interact with others. Life is what you make of it. You *can* create your destiny. Look at it like this, your experience has given you valuable insights about life, the nature of human beings, and the importance of knowing where you come from. The point is, you know what it feels like to not have a parent or both, be there for you. This perspective is very powerful because it enables you to know just how important it is to show the trusted people in your life how much you love and appreciate them.

Your child is rebelling. Consider the following,

A) Take some time to understand why your child is acting out.

B) Rebelling is a normal part of human development.

Takeaway: Most parents do the best they can to raise their child or children and provide for them. As children grow up, they begin to question everything, including whether their parents know best. Children are on their own path to figuring out who they are and often go through a rebellious phase, so if their rebellious actions are not frequent and/or reckless, cut them some slack. Instead of punishing your child for their rebellious actions, take some time to understand why your child is acting out and what might be bothering him or her.

Your family is constantly putting you down. Consider the following,

A) Some people manifest their anger in different ways.

B) A heart-to-heart conversation can be helpful.

Takeaway: Family should serve as a source of inspiration, strength and support for all members of the unit. When there is friction among families, no one benefits and all suffer in one way or another. When your family is ganging up on you or constantly putting you down, take a step back and try to keep your composure. If you are able to, sit them down and have a discussion about your feelings and concerns. If an open and honest conversation does not do the trick, then maybe professional help could be of better assistance.

Your relationship with your sibling(s) has gone downhill. Consider the following,

A) Communication is important when trying to maintain healthy relationships.

B) Not all family members get along.

Takeaway: There is a saying, "blood is thicker than water," but sometimes that is not the case and siblings grow apart, for reasons known and unknown. Every relationship is a two-way street, meaning both parties have to come together to make the relationship work. If the opportunity arises where you can sit down and talk honestly then, by all means, do so. If you both decide your relationship is irreparable, it could be better to let bygones be bygones.

You were adopted and do not know your birth parents. Consider the following,

A) Be thankful if you were adopted by parents who love and care for you.

B) Sometimes the past belongs in the past.

Takeaway: When biological parents feel they are unable to raise a child, they choose adoption as a means to ensure the child is properly cared for. Just because you were adopted and do not know your birth parents does not mean you are lacking in love or anything else in life. If you are really curious about your birth parents, then attempt the search yourself or hire experts to help you. If you were adopted by loving parents who have selflessly cared for you, a) be thankful that was the case and b) your parents will understand, but it could be helpful to let them know how much they mean to you and that even if your search is fruitful, nothing or no one will replace the love you have for them in your heart. If you were not as lucky to be adopted by loving parents, it does not make you inferior or incomplete in any way.

Your child and new partner do not get along. Consider the following,

A) Developing an honest dialogue is essential if you want to cultivate healthy relationships.

B) Learning about each other's commonalities can be helpful in becoming closer.

Takeaway: Healthy relationships are cultivated through the development of honest, ongoing dialogues between people about how they feel. If you typically have a good relationship with your child and value that relationship, then you will do everything in your power to make this situation work. For instance, schedule a group session with a therapist or participate in a group activity that brings you all closer. If your child is an adult with a life of their own, have an honest conversation with them about why you like being with this person and hopefully they may come around.

Your nanny is emotionally closer to your children than you are. Consider the following,

A) As a parent, it is your responsibility to create a loving environment for your children.

B) Nannies can be replaced.

Takeaway: You have an obligation to create a loving and nurturing environment for your children, after all, you are the parent. If you are too busy with work, try to set aside time to spend with your children doing activities you all enjoy. If you have hired a nanny to care for your children while you are at work, know that this is not a bad choice and shows that you care about them. However, children do establish bonds with people who genuinely invest time in getting to know them. If the concept of your nanny being closer to your children is bothering you, keep in mind your nanny does not have to be a permanent fixture in your family and even though finding trustworthy nannies can be difficult, it is not impossible.

A family member repeatedly asks you for money.
Consider the following,

A) Lending money to loved ones can be tricky.

B) There are other ways you can help.

Takeaway: Money-matters are always a subject of scrutiny. If a loved one asks to borrow money and you say "no," then you are considered a jerk. If you say "yes" and ask for repayment, then you are considered a jerk. It is never a win-win situation. It is always best to help the people you love and care for, but if you are not in a good position financially to help yourself, then you certainly cannot help others. On the other hand, if you helped out and have not received repayment, it is important to have a discussion with this person to figure out a repayment plan. If your attempts to discuss the situation are unsuccessful, you may have to cut your losses or take legal action if it is a substantial amount of money. In the future, when lending money to anyone, begin the process by drafting a contract that details a plan of repayment, including the amount being loaned, interest if applicable and when the loan should be repaid.

Your child had an unethical relationship with a teacher. Consider the following,

A) Any adult who engages in an unethical relationship with a minor is a predator and should be reported.

B) It is a parent's responsibility to ensure their children are safe.

Takeaway: As a parent, you do everything in your power to protect and nurture your child so they can lead a good life. Knowing that your child was taken advantage of by someone you entrusted to care for them is heartbreaking. The teacher—an adult—should have known better. Children, no matter how mature they seem, are still developing, mentally, physically and emotionally. Do not feel bad for alerting the school or the authorities about this unethical relationship, you have nothing to feel guilty about. As much as you may want to take this situation into your own hands, think of the consequences, you may end up doing more harm than good. The main goal now is to help your child heal, and professional counseling can be a good starting point.

Your child came out as being gay. Consider the following,

A) A parent's love should be given unconditionally.

B) Learn to accept your child's sexuality.

Takeaway: Love is a powerful emotion. It is powerful enough to inspire people to climb the highest mountain or cross a raging sea.

So, when two people are drawn toward each other, it is very hard to break them apart. Though it can be difficult to understand the dynamics of a same-sex relationship, do not shun your child because you do not understand their choices. This choice does not change who they are as a person. The choice they made was to be true to who they are and what they feel in their heart, and that is a very courageous action.

Your child is dating or marrying a person you do not approve of. Consider the following,

A) Be happy if your child is happy.

B) Get to know your child's partner and learn what makes them special.

Takeaway: Parents often have a vision of the type of person they hope their child meets and when reality does not match the dream, it can result in feelings of dislike. In fact, there may be several reasons why you do not approve of or like your child's partner. However, the worst decision you can make is to shut your child out; support is better than shunning. Sometimes we have to put our personal views aside and support the people we love and try to make it work. Your main concern should be to support your child.

Your blended-family is not blending well. Consider the following,

A) All families, including blended-families, are full of people with different personalities.

B) Every member of the family plays an active role in making this new family dynamic work.

Takeaway: Parents play a huge role in facilitating family dynamics and making children feel comfortable. It is always best not to catch your children off-guard in this type of situation or any situation for that matter. A proper discussion, officiated by both parents, is important prior to introducing your children to a whole new family dynamic. If your new family dynamic is not blending as smoothly as you hoped, there are tools and resources, such as professional counseling and support groups, available to help you instill balance and create stability within this new blended-family.

CHAPTER 2

FRIENDS

"One loyal friend is worth ten thousand relatives."
–Euripides

There is a saying, "you can't choose your family but you can choose your friends." Good friends are hard to come by but that does not mean they do not exist. All friendships are different because no two people are alike, and every friendship experiences ups and downs.

In fact, the success of any relationship, romantic or platonic, is based on developing a solid, underlying friendship that meets the needs of both people. Cultivating a healthy, dependable, close relationship with a friend can certainly enhance any person's life. Healthy friendships have these traits in common; equal amounts of give and take, comfortability in sharing, development of trust, moments of laughter and rejoicing, and shared interests—and if you don't have these traits in your friendship, then it isn't a solid friendship.

In reality, every person we meet can teach us a lesson. Sometimes people are in our lives for a reason, season or lifetime. Regardless of the amount of time a friendship lasts, it is important to cherish the good moments and learn from every lesson presented.

Life is about learning lessons and our friendships can teach us more about ourselves, about other people, and the nature of human behavior. For example, what if a friend betrayed you? Or you confided to someone you thought was your friend? The emotions you may be feeling, like betrayal or anger, could overpower your good judgment. The Mental Health Foundation advises in their Boiling Point report, one in five people say they have ended a relationship or friendship with someone because of how they behaved when they were angry.

There are times when close friends approach different stages in their lives and that is normal, but if you have to put extra effort into making a friendship work or are struggling to find common ground, perhaps it's time to move on. You are in control of who you let into your life and who you choose to let go of.

Be thankful for the friends in your life. Be thankful for the friends you have been able to weed out of your life. Be thankful for every lesson you have learned. Our growth as human beings is only possible if we learn from our experiences and overcome similar situations in the future.

A friend betrayed you. Consider the following,

A) They probably were not your friend to begin with.

B) If they did it to you, it is likely they may do it to someone else.

Takeaway: True friends have a genuine interest in the well-being of the people they care about. If a friend has demonstrated in some way or another that they cannot be trusted, then count your blessings that you found out when you did. It does not matter if this was a 1-year friendship or a 10-year friendship; you are now the wiser, so revel in knowing that. There is also no need to stoop to their level and retaliate or get even. We all reap what we sow.

You and your best friend are not close anymore. Consider the following,

A) Friendships, like all relationships, go through phases.

B) Dwindling friendships can be revived.

Takeaway: Cultivating healthy friendships and relationships is an essential component to human development. Like all relationships, friendships also go through phases. However, if two people are sincere about their friendship with one another, they will make the time to clear the air and mend the friendship if need be. Keep in mind that as people age, their responsibilities increase which often outweighs making time to spend with friends. At some point, if the relationship is truly solid, it will all work itself out. In the meantime, focus on what makes *you* happy.

Your friends are talking about you behind your back.
Consider the following,

A)   Gossip is a part of human nature.

B)   True friends will address their concerns to your face.

Takeaway: Have confidence in who you are as a person. Though it can be hurtful when you find out that your friends are talking negatively about you, it is important to evaluate who you are hanging out with. Chances are, if your friends typically talk negatively about other people, at some point they may talk negatively about you. You may want to find a different circle of friends who focus more on the positive than the negative.

You confided to a person you thought was your friend.
Consider the following,

A)   Sometimes it is better to keep your thoughts and opinions to yourself.

B)   Trust takes time to build.

Takeaway: It would be great to be able to take people at face value, however, some people are only concerned about themselves. Some people can be trusted and others cannot. If you confided your thoughts or opinions to someone you thought was your friend or had your best interest at heart and found out otherwise, take it as a lesson well learned and make sure not to repeat it in the future. Always keep in mind that trust must be earned, and to earn trust, takes time.

Your friends stopped talking to each other and you are in the middle. Consider the following,

A) A true friend would never make you choose sides.

B) Do not put yourself in a predicament where both friends are confiding to you about the other.

Takeaway: True friends would not put you in a situation where you must choose sides. If you were not a part of their falling out, then their issues should not affect you. If you remain friends with both parties, make sure you are not placed in a compromising situation where they are sharing their views about the other to you. This can create problems because, first off, you are not a mediator and hearing their frustrations could lead to you becoming biased. Stay neutral in this situation and if it is clear that they want to involve you, then neither has your best interest at heart.

A friend has not returned your belongings. Consider the following,

A) Do not lend possessions that you cannot afford to part with.

B) Some people are not as mindful about returning items they lent or borrowed in a timely manner.

Takeaway: Do not take it personally if your friend has not returned your possessions. Some people are not as good as others when it comes to returning items. If you know your friend is not good at returning what they lent or borrowed, this could be a factor in helping you decide if you really want to lend your items. If the item in question has value to you, that could also be another factor that aides your decision. You do not have to lend anything to anyone if you do not feel comfortable about it. If you are still waiting for your item to be returned, remind your friend to bring your item the next time you get together or coordinate a time to pass by their house and pick it up if it means that much to you.

You hosted a friend at your house and they were high-maintenance and/or inconsiderate. Consider the following,

A) Try to be a hospitable host.

B) Everyone is accustomed to certain comforts and quality of life, try not to judge them.

Takeaway: Some people are mindful guests and others are not. When deciding on accommodating friends or guests at your home, make your decision wisely because having an inconsiderate guest in your home can impact your daily life and routine. If your friend or guest lacks the foresight to be helpful, then just make a mental note of it for the future. Also, think twice about being too accommodating to people you do not know too much about. All-in-all, you do not have to let this experience affect your friendship, just be wiser in the future about who you invite to stay in your home.

You pet-sat for a friend and the pet destroyed your home. Consider the following,

A) Find out the pet's history first.

B) If you have a pet-free home, you may want to keep it that way.

Takeaway: When helping out a friend by taking care of their pet(s), it is essential to begin the dialogue with understanding the pet's history and routine. Learning about a pet's routine can be a helpful indicator as to whether you will be able to care for it the way it is accustomed to being cared for. And if you own pets, you will also need to consider if all the pets will get along. This is also true if you have young children. Your safety and your family's safety should be the primary concern. If you have a pet-free home, then you may want to keep it that way. Pets, just like humans, may not adjust well in unfamiliar surroundings. If the pet caused significant damage to your home, then it could be worthwhile to discuss it with your friend and agree upon a suitable solution. Just tread carefully, and learn from your past decisions.

Your best friend and partner do not get along. Consider the following,

A) Not all people and personalities mesh well together.

B) You should not have to choose between keeping your friendship or relationship.

Takeaway: Not all people get along, unfortunately. It could simply boil down to incompatible personalities or delve deeper into some other issue. It is not an ideal situation to be in when your best friend and partner do not get along. In situations like this, you should not have to choose between keeping your friendship or staying in your relationship. You should be able to spend time with each person independently without receiving any sort of backlash.

A friend talks negatively about everyone and everything in his or her life. Consider the following,

A) Some people just need to vent.

B) Some people have toxic energy.

Takeaway: In this situation, there are two types of people. The first type, are the people who get frustrated with the people in their life because they do not know how to stand up for themselves, therefore they vent, and the second type are people with toxic energy who bad-mouth others. If you have a genuine interest in the people you care about, then you will offer support and lend a listening ear to your friends. However, when people constantly express negative sentiment, it can become difficult to be around them. If your friend is coming from a genuine place, it could be worthwhile for them to speak to a therapist who could help them become more vocal about their concerns. If your friend is not coming from a genuine place, maybe you should consider limiting your interaction with them and/or assess if they are a friend worth keeping.

A friend stole from you. Consider the following,

A)   This is an indicator that shows you this person is not your friend.

B)   Do not resort to violence to retrieve your possession.

Takeaway: When personal possessions are stolen, it can bring up many emotions, especially emotions of anger and loss. Human beings attach themselves to material possessions for one reason or another. It is OK if that is the case but be mindful in knowing that our possessions do not make us who we are. Our possessions have no value to us once we pass away either. If the item makes no real difference in your life, chalk up the situation as a lesson well learned. If the possession is valuable, it is worth reporting it to the police. Do not resort to taking matters into your own hands. You never know the outcome of any given situation and violence never solves anything.

A friend asks you for a lot more than you get in return.
Consider the following,

A) Some people seek support from friends because family may not be able to help.

B) If there is a clear disparity in the friendship, this may not be a genuine friend.

Takeaway: Friendships should have an equal amount of give and take. When a friend asks you for more than you get in return, it is worthwhile to assess why this is happening. For instance, some people seek comfort and support from friends because their family or loved ones may not be able to help them. Other people may leech off of friends and take advantage of their kindness. So it is up to you to figure out what type of friendship this is—genuine or disingenuous—and make a decision to continue or cut the friendship.

You feel left out of group activities with friends.
Consider the following,

A) Get involved in your community by joining clubs, attending classes or volunteering for a noble cause.

B) Make new friends.

Takeaway: Having a stable social circle of trusted friends is important. However, when people feel excluded from group activities, especially in social settings, it can create feelings of anger, vulnerability and insecurity. Regardless of being left out intentionally or unintentionally, take this as an opportunity to get out of your comfort zone and expand your horizons by creating more options for yourself. When we place all of our eggs in one basket, we could be disappointed by the outcome if that basket falls. Getting involved in the community, joining clubs and organizations that peak your interest, or attending classes and seminars, can help you meet other like-minded individuals, further enriching your life.

A friend keeps canceling plans. Consider the following,

A) Do not take it personally.

B) Try to make spontaneous plans.

Takeaway: Coordinating plans with a friend or even a group of friends can be difficult because each person involved has a different set of priorities and responsibilities that can interfere with plans scheduled on leisure time. Do not take it personally if the plans you make with a friend keep getting canceled. If you are constantly being flexible and accommodating your friend and they disregard your time and schedule, then take it as a sign that they have other priorities. However, if you are both equally to blame, then just be understanding that life cannot always be planned and sometimes spontaneity is the perfect solution.

A friend is dating or involved with your ex-partner. Consider the following,

A) It is natural to feel upset, but for your own peace of mind, it is best to let go of those feelings.

B) If they are happy together, then be happy for them.

Takeaway: Relationships—romantic or platonic—are not easy, period. It could be that you have many questions about how these two people got together, and that is normal. If a close friend, who truly values your friendship, is dating your ex-partner, he or she will be chivalrous enough to talk to you about it. Typically, other people's love lives are their business, not anyone else's—especially if they are not causing any harm. Fact is, you and your ex-partner are no longer together and there has to be a reason for that. If the couple is happy then be happy for them. Do your best to let go of any negative emotions you may be harboring and move forward with your life by enriching it with people and activities you enjoy.

CHAPTER 3

ROMANCE

"You don't develop courage by being happy in your relationships every day. You develop it by surviving difficult times and challenging adversity."
–Epicurus

W hat is life without love? Is it better to have loved than to never have loved at all? These are some of the age-old questions that people have asked when pondering the relevancy of romantic relationships.

We all seek companionship, unconditional love and acceptance, and emotional security in our relationships, along with other traits like trust and attraction. Having desires in your relationship and expectations of your partner is natural. In fact, healthy relationships have an equal amount of give and take. Besides that, relationships are more enjoyable when you're partnered with someone who enriches your life, regardless of having shared interests—which does help too.

There is an inner contentment people feel when they are in love, and especially when their needs are being met. However, feelings of uncertainty can arise when a person's needs are not being met. People's mindset and expectations change over time, mainly because people and relationships are bound to evolve at one point or another. For example, what happens when your partner cheats on you, or you feel like you are not getting enough attention in your relationship? Maybe you want to get married but your partner does not? The answers to these questions are serious, mainly because anything that tugs at our heartstrings is not something to be taken light-heartedly.

Fact is, your perception about life and the experiences you go through will never mirror your partner's perception because you are entirely different people. Your life history and accumulation of experiences are different. In addition to that, you are genetically, psychologically and physiologically different too, which is why compromise and mutual understanding are important factors to the success of any relationship.

In any case, romantic relationships can bring happiness as well as heartbreak, just like anything in life. However, there is something very special about being in love and if you are lucky to experience it, cherish it for everything it is worth. Most people who have experienced love know there is nothing logical about it. Every relationship experiences trials and tribulations. As long as your partner's quirks are not abusive or destructive in nature, disagreements can certainly be overcome. It's how you handle these moments that makes your bond stronger and your love truly worthwhile.

You were dumped. Consider the following,

A) Everyone experiences being rejected at least once in their lifetime.

B) Each relationship in our life helps us to better prepare for the right one.

Takeaway: People become attached to comfort or what is most familiar to them. The hardest aspect of breaking up is losing a routine that you were accustomed to. Cherish the memories and good times you shared with this person, and learn from past mistakes. Change is good because with it comes a different perspective, and perspective is everything especially if you want to make the best out of life. There is a saying, "there are plenty of fish in the sea," meaning, you have plenty of options regardless of whether you see them or not.

You and your partner got into an argument and are not speaking to each other. Consider the following,

A) An argument does not constitute the end of the world.

B) Take some time to cool off before addressing your frustrations.

Takeaway: When heated discussions arise, it is better for both parties to simply walk away and agree to resume a non-confrontational discussion at a later time and/or day. Comments said out of spite can be hurtful. The point of a discussion is to work out an effective solution. If for any reason your argument leads to violence, then this is not a good situation. Volatile relationships are not worth the consequences. In cases like that, you should distance yourself immediately and seek professional help to begin the healing process.

You are not getting enough attention in your relationship. Consider the following,

A) Feeling cared for and loved by your partner is important in any relationship.

B) Spending quality time to get to know your partner is vital.

Takeaway: Spending quality time together is beneficial for both individuals in the relationship. If the relationship seems one-sided, it is important to evaluate if this is something you can accept or deal with. Whatever the reasons may be, if you are not getting enough attention from your partner, it is important to communicate that to them. Let them know your concerns and designate time to spend with one another, free from outside distractions. If your partner is not open to this, then you have your answer.

Your partner is emotionally unavailable. Consider the following,

A) Emotional security is an important aspect of a healthy relationship.

B) Make sure your needs are being met.

Takeaway: Emotional security is a fundamental aspect of any successful and healthy relationship. Being in a relationship where your emotional needs are not being met can be psychologically and physically draining. When a person truly wants to be with you, you will have no doubt that they are there for you. You will not have to fight to be heard, you will not have to go beyond your comfort zone to feel this security that you are currently lacking. It is hard to accept when the relationship you are in may not be worth the effort especially if you have put in extra effort to make the relationship work. In all honesty, you cannot force someone to give you the security you need. It could be beneficial to sum up your efforts as a job well done and move on to greener pastures.

You are cheating on your partner. Consider the following,

A) Do not be in a monogamous relationship if you cannot commit.

B) If you are not happy in your relationship, then share your feelings with your partner.

Takeaway: When two people decide to be in an exclusive, monogamous relationship, it is typically because they have no inclination to want to see anyone else. If you are unhappy in your relationship for one reason or another, you owe it to yourself and your partner to be honest about how you feel. Cheating on your partner is not fair to him or her, nor is it fair to your relationship. If your partner finds out, you may have difficulty in repairing the trust you lost.

You love your partner but still think about your ex-partner. Consider the following,

A) You are not fully invested in your partner.

B) It is not fair to string someone along.

Takeaway: We tend to develop feelings for people we spend a lot of time with, this is especially true of relationships. Sometimes, even though we break up with someone we dated, we still have feelings for them and that is OK. However, if you are still thinking about your ex-partner, then you are not fully invested in your current partner or relationship. This is a problem because you will not be able to fully focus your attention and love on the person who is investing their time and energy on you, in the now. You owe it to your partner to not string them along or to resolve your feelings and fully commit to your partner moving forward.

Your partner is abusive. Consider the following,

A) There is no valid reason that can justify staying in an abusive relationship.

B) Your partner has a problem that only a professional can help with.

Takeaway: There is no valid reason that can justify staying in an abusive relationship or a reason to validate the abuse. If your partner is physically, verbally and/or emotionally abusive, you owe it to yourself to get out of the situation immediately. Some people get off on putting others down. Their own insecurities drive them to demoralize those around them who exude confidence. When people take out their anger in an aggressive and violent manner, they are not only a danger to everyone in their presence but also to themselves. This is a problem that cannot be fixed by you, it can only be fixed by getting them professional help.

Your partner has a wandering eye or acts overly flirtatious. Consider the following,

A) It is disrespectful to your partner to invest energy and attention on other people.

B) Your partner may not be fully committed to you.

Takeaway: Some people's personalities can be perceived as flirtatious and others downright crave attention. However, if you are in a monogamous relationship and your partner has a constant wandering eye or acts overly flirtatious, besides appearing disrespectful, it could be a tell-tale sign of someone who is not 100 percent invested in you. If you are bothered by your partner's wandering eye or flirty attitude, share your concern with him or her. Ideally, your partner will respect how you feel and improve his or her behavior, otherwise, you may have to consider sucking it up and overlooking it or breaking up.

You contracted a sexually transmitted infection (STI). Consider the following,

A) Your health should be your primary concern.

B) Always use protection.

Takeaway: Your health and well-being should be your first priority. Protected sex, though not 100 percent effective against pregnancies and STIs, is the best option. Getting yearly checkups to ensure a clean bill of health is highly advised for your own peace of mind. Putting aside how you got into the situation, consensual or nonconsensual, be thankful if you contracted an STI that is curable. If you contracted an STI that is incurable, know that this is not the end of your life. Modern day medicine can provide comfort and prevent further damage to your health. There are support groups available to help you work through your grief or shame. You can lead a normal life but you have to believe that in order for it to happen.

Your partner misled you about the seriousness of your relationship. Consider the following,

A) Do not blame yourself for trusting your partner.

B) Do not allow yourself to be strung along.

Takeaway: We tend to invest a lot of our time and energy into the people we are dating, especially if we can picture a future with them. If you are in a relationship and were misled about its seriousness, it is imperative to reevaluate what you want. Being in a dead-end relationship will not get you anywhere. It is very easy to become comfortable in established routines and there is nothing wrong in being too comfortable but when that comfort inhibits you from fulfilling your needs then you are doing yourself a disservice. If you are unhappy in your situation, then you owe it to yourself to do what makes you happy and if that means breaking up, then so be it.

You do not trust your partner anymore. Consider the following,

A) Trust is very important in any relationship.

B) Understanding why you feel this way will help you assess the situation.

Takeaway: Trust is an essential component to any successful relationship and must be earned. Giving away your trust prematurely in any situation can have negative repercussions but that does not mean it is always the case. First, it is important to understand why you feel this way, either through self-evaluation or through professional help, like a session or two with a therapist or life coach. Once you are able to understand why you feel this way, then you can make a better decision based upon your findings to either work on strengthening your relationship or break up.

Your partner is cheating on you. Consider the following,

A) All relationships go through trials and tribulations.

B) You can choose to work it out or break up.

Takeaway: When a person cheats, it is because there is a deeper issue at stake, like not being interested anymore or not being ready for a serious commitment. Whatever the reason is, it could be worth it to hear your partner's concerns, if that option is available. All relationships go through their own trials and tribulations. If you both want the relationship to succeed, then work hard at repairing it. If you are certain this relationship is beyond repair or not what you envisioned, then it might be wise to break up, hopefully under amicable circumstances.

Your spouse wants a divorce. Consider the following,

A) Some relationships just do not work out.

B) You are not a failure because your marriage did not succeed.

Takeaway: It seems like a large majority of marriages in America end in divorce these days. Fact is entering into marriage is a decision that should be well thought out. In any case, some relationships do not work out in the long run, and that is OK. Getting divorced does not mean you failed to make your relationship work. However, it could be beneficial to take the time to speak to a professional who can help you process this life event for what it is. Now is the moment for healing and when you do heal from this, there is always another chance at finding love no matter your age.

Your long-distance relationship is not working out. Consider the following,

A) Some people can manage a long distance relationship and others cannot.

B) You can still be friends.

Takeaway: Being in a long-distance relationship can be tricky because you miss out on opportunities to be with your partner in person. Learning about your partner through shared experiences and face-to-face interaction is important in understanding who your partner is, what their values are and figuring out if you are compatible. Just because your relationship could not withstand the distance does not mean the love was not there. Love is powerful and when it is genuine, nothing can change its course. If you can maintain a friendship instead, then great, it is still a win-win situation.

You are not in love with your partner anymore. Consider the following,

A) It is not uncommon to fall out of love.

B) It is always best to communicate your feelings with your partner.

Takeaway: We all hope to find everlasting love at some point in our lives. Communicating your feelings to your partner, throughout the course of your relationship, is really important. It is important for a couple of reasons, a) so that you are both on the same page and b) so you do not mislead or catch your partner off-guard about how you feel. Love is a powerful emotion but if you do not feel as deeply about your partner as they do about you, then you owe it to them and yourself to be honest.

CHAPTER 4

HOME

*"The strength of a nation derives from
the integrity of the home."*
–Confucius

"Home is where the heart is," we have all heard this expression in one context or another and know it bears validity. Everything about a person's home is personal, to them, and there is nothing wrong with that. Most people get a feeling of security when at home. It is a place associated with comfort, and most of all, you.

The environment we are in affects us emotionally and psychologically. Architects and interior designers agree that space has a direct impact on how we feel and how we perform, consciously and subconsciously. As a matter of fact, evidence-based research by neuroscientists and psychologists infers that the way we design and decorate our home affects our health, productivity and self-worth, including our ability to make decisions and react to life happenings. If designed thoughtfully, our dwelling has the power to promote mind and body wellness.

No matter where a person lives—an apartment, a housing complex or a private residence—home-related issues will pop up from time to time. The maintenance and upkeep of a home is a big responsibility that comes with other burdens, all of which can be fixed. Maybe you're dealing with defiant tenants, weather damage or pest infestations, or going through a foreclosure. Juggling one or all of these issues can be overwhelming especially if you have other pressing priorities.

In actuality, most of us are very lucky to be living in a country that has a stable infrastructure. There are people living in other parts of the world that are not as privileged and live with far less. For instance, some people do not have a place to live and others may not be equipped with amenities such as clean water, air conditioning or even electricity.

A big part of life is how we deal with our problems. Do not allow low-level priorities to get the best of you. Be thankful for what you have; a home, a job, food in the fridge and other luxuries we may take for granted. If your dwelling is creating more issues for you, then think of solutions to overcome them while preserving your sanity.

If we know that space influences how we feel then we should consciously create a space that's pleasing to our mind and body, thereby encouraging a more meaningful, fulfilling and joyful experience. In fact, this concept of manipulating aesthetic elements to influence our mood and well-being has proven data that shows it inspires unity, fosters learning, and promotes social and personal growth, and would be highly beneficial in places where feeling inspired and accepted is fundamental to the success of the community like schools, work and even lower income housing.

Your property sustained damage and requires costly repairs. Consider the following,

A) Property damage, at some point, is inevitable.

B) Figure out a reasonable budget for repairs and aim to stick to it.

Takeaway: There are many upsides to owning a home or an apartment. However, part of the downside is that the owner is responsible for paying for repairs or improvements. If your property was damaged for one reason or another, try not to get too upset about it. The main goal should be how you can fix the issue within your budget. Check to see if your homeowners or renters insurance policy covers the damages, or if an environmental issue needs to be brought to your adjustor's attention. If legal action needs to be taken, then be prepared to go through the motions.

Your neighbor is not considerate of others. Consider the following,

A) Some people are so focused on themselves they forget their actions impact others around them.

B) Part of being a functioning member of society is coping with people you may not otherwise interact with.

Takeaway: Neighbors, as nice or mean as they may be, are human just like you and me. They have their good days and they have their bad days. At the end of the day, we are all living life for ourselves. Some people may not be as mindful as others. In a situation where your neighbor has done something to upset you, calmly bring it up to them and find a solution, if possible. Do not approach the situation as if it were a confrontation because you will not get anywhere. Be kind and understanding and most of all, try to be neighborly.

Neighborhood kids vandalized your property. Consider the following,

A) Report the incident to the police immediately.

B) Do not retaliate.

Takeaway: Kids are inexperienced in life and they make poor decisions because they do not think about the consequences associated with their actions. Even though you are rightfully upset about the damage caused to your property, do not take it upon yourself to seek justice. Taking the law into your own hands can have far greater consequences than the destruction of your property. If the vandalism is taking place while you are at home, call the police immediately and do not go outside. You never know the temperament of other people. If you were not home at the time of the vandalism, call the police and do not touch anything.

Your house was destroyed by someone you entrusted its care to. Consider the following,

A) File an incident report with the police if applicable.

B) A house can always be repaired.

Takeaway: There are a couple of common reasons people entrust the care of their home to someone else, a) they are unable to care for the home or b) they rented it out short-term to make extra money. If your home was destroyed by someone you entrusted its care to, the first step would be to take photos of the damage. Depending on the circumstances, figure out your options for reporting the incident. If you are able to come up with an agreement for reimbursement of damages, then great, just make sure you get it in writing. In fact, an agreement beforehand is ideal. All in all, rest assured, a damaged house can always be repaired.

A car is parked in your assigned parking space. Consider the following,

A) Take the appropriate measures to report the problem.

B) Remain calm and park somewhere else temporarily.

Takeaway: It can be very frustrating when your assigned parking space is occupied by someone else. It is best to remain calm and do not appear upset, outwardly. If you live in an apartment, notify the front desk attendant so they can take the appropriate measures to have the car moved or towed, if that is their policy. Do not take matters into your own hands by causing damage to another person's car. If the driver is around, be polite and let them know the parking spaces are assigned and as an added goodwill gesture, let them know where the guest parking is located. For all you know, it could have been a simple mistake.

You cannot afford to pay your rent or are being evicted or foreclosed on. Consider the following,

A) Be realistic about your financial situation.

B) Figure out legal solutions to solve your problem.

Takeaway: Be realistic about your financial situation. Budget wisely and when you are searching for a place to live, remember to live within your means. When you are unable to pay your rent, speak with your landlord about your dilemma and try to work out a payment plan. If you are being evicted or foreclosed on, figure out a legal solution to solve your problem. There is always a solution to every problem. If you are unable to think of a plan that can help, find another suitable living arrangement, like staying with family or friends, and perhaps explore your job options to improve your income.

Your house has a pest infestation. Consider the following,

A) Hire an exterminator to solve your problem.

B) Attempt to resolve the problem yourself.

Takeaway: Pest infestations can be a tremendous nuisance and can be an added level of stress on your full plate of responsibilities. When situations like this occur, it could be one of two reasons causing this, a) structural issues like gaps that are giving the pests an entryway and/or b) there is a food source they are drawn to. By figuring out the source of your problem, you can then easily figure out a solution like hiring a pest control company or handling the issue yourself.

Your tenants are a nightmare to deal with. Consider the following,

A) Try to be patient when interacting with them.

B) If your tenants are violating clauses in your agreement, take the appropriate measures to evict them.

Takeaway: Landlords are, by law, required to ensure that their rental property is in accordance with the rules and regulations set forth regarding minimum health, safety, housing and maintenance standards, and it is the landlord's responsibility to make sure they do not deteriorate below these standards. Additionally, tenants deserve a chance to prove they can commit to the agreement they signed. If after a reasonable amount of time you realize that your tenants are not exactly what you expected, it is only fair to remind them about the contract they signed with you. You can point out what they agreed to, perhaps keeping the place neat, not having pets, whatever it is they are doing that they agreed not to do. If they continue to disregard the rules, your best option is to evict them. Take the appropriate legal route if necessary and do not feel like you are overreacting or being overly cautious.

Your roommate unexpectedly moved out. Consider the following,

A) Try to understand their point of view.

B) Begin the process to find a new roommate, if necessary.

Takeaway: Having a roommate can be lots of fun or cause for a huge headache. When a roommate unexpectedly moves out, it can cause you to rethink your relationship with this person, your living arrangement or even your financial security and can bring about many different emotions. Try to be mindful that people have their own reasoning, which can appear selfish to you but worthwhile and necessary to them. You probably have a roommate because it relieves certain pressures off of you. By them moving out, you will have to rethink how you will be able to manage everything from a financial standpoint, and maybe even a domestic standpoint too. Put effort into finding a new roommate, as tedious and bothersome as it may be. By exploring these options, you should be able to find a suitable solution. Keep in mind that results have a direct correlation to the effort we put into the task at hand.

You have been displaced from your home. Consider the following,

A) Stay with family or friends temporarily.

B) Be calm and methodical when exploring your options.

Takeaway: We are all subject to experience social, economic and environmental-related issues that can impact our way of life. If you have been displaced from your home due to environmental issues or housing reasons, find out if you can stay with family or friends temporarily while you explore your options. Be methodical and strategic with how you approach this situation. For instance, find out if your homeowners or renters insurance policy covers the issue you may be having or if there are organizations that can provide aid or relief.

Your landlord is not helpful and/or rude. Consider the following,

A) If your landlord is breaching your contract, consider exploring your legal options.

B) Find somewhere else to live.

Takeaway: Developing a healthy and functional landlord-tenant relationship is very important especially if you want to live in peace. Renters are obligated to pay their rent on time, behave well, keep the property clean, and notify the landlord in a timely manner of damages that require repair. If your landlord is not helpful and neglects to fulfill certain obligations outlined in your contract like not fostering a habitable space, consider exploring your legal options. If your landlord does fulfill his or her responsibilities but is rude or unpleasant to deal with, try to be mindful that some people may not be friendly and be thankful they are not neglecting their duties. If that type of relationship causes you stress, you may have to consider living elsewhere.

You are having difficulty selling your house. Consider the following,

A) Make sure your listing price is reasonable.

B) Making minor improvements can improve your chances of attracting a serious buyer.

Takeaway: Selling a house is generally a tedious, multi-level process, full of many stresses. If you are having difficulty selling your house, make sure your listing price is comparable to market value. Sometimes, it helps to know the prices of other houses for sale in your neighborhood to confirm your listing price is considered reasonable. Also, by making minor improvements to your house, you can improve your chances of attracting a serious buyer. For instance, stage the inside of your house to highlight the house's main selling points or enhance the landscape, especially in the front of your house. Most of all, have patience and remember to be optimistic.

A neighbor's party is getting loud and rowdy. Consider the following,

A) Be flexible, let people have fun once in a while.

B) If damage is being caused, call the police.

Takeaway: We all need a little fun in our lives and moments of celebration and rejoicing bring happiness. If your neighbors do not have loud and rowdy parties frequently, you may want to allow them to have their fun, maybe at the expense of a night not well slept. If physical damage is being caused to the property or surrounding properties, then it could be worth it to notify the police. Do not take measures into your own hands to break up the party, especially if you are agitated. If you are on good terms with your neighbor, you may want to call or text them and politely let them know that the party is becoming too loud.

Your house was robbed. Consider the following,

A) Possessions can always be replaced.

B) Homeowners or renters insurance policies can be beneficial to have.

Takeaway: A home is a very personal and intimate space, so when burglars break into a home, steal possessions and/or ransack the space, it can cause the homeowner and other occupants to feel unsafe and angry. If your home was robbed and everyone is OK, then do not dwell on a situation that was ultimately beyond your control. Call the police and file a report. Hopefully, you have homeowners or renters insurance to help you recover any damages caused to your home. If priceless family heirlooms were stolen, do your best not to dwell on it. Although dealing with this situation can be more of a headache, be thankful nothing worse happened. It could be worthwhile to explore your home-security options like installing an alarm or cameras or even consider getting a dog, to help you feel safe.

You are ashamed of your house and do not bring anyone over. Consider the following,

A) Genuine people will not judge you based on the appearance of your house.

B) If your house is filthy, you are doing yourself a major disservice.

Takeaway: A person's home is very special because it is a reflection of the homeowner's style, personality and habits. If you are ashamed of your house because it is cluttered with junk and/or filthy, you owe it to your mental and physical health to clean up your home. If the task is too overwhelming, then call cleaning experts and pay them to help you. If you are ashamed because you do not own expensive furniture, do not worry too much because genuine people will not judge you based on what you own.

CHAPTER 5

WORK

*"There is one thing one has to have,
either a soul that is cheerful by nature or a soul
made cheerful by work, love, art and knowledge."*
–Friedrich Nietzsche

Most people spend the majority of their day at work, in the company of people with different personalities they may or may not ordinarily surround themselves with. Keeping that in mind, it can be easy to understand how problems and obstacles at work could contribute to a person's level of stress. For example, conflict with your boss can lead to thoughts of quitting. Being unexpectedly fired can lead to thoughts of uncertainty, and all of these thoughts and the feelings they elicit can cause anxiety and lead to a negative perception of life.

A report issued by ComPsych, a global provider of employee assistance programs, suggests the main causes of workplace stress are primarily due to workload (41%), people issues (32%), juggling work and personal lives (18%), and lack of job security (9%). The American Institute of Stress indicated that 80 percent of workers feel stress on the job and nearly half say they need help in learning how to manage stress.

Chronic stress can lead to an assortment of health problems. According to scientists at Duke Medicine, a genetic trait known to make some people especially sensitive to stress also appears to be responsible for a 38 percent increased risk of having a heart attack or death in patients with heart disease. Additionally, when we can't manage stress, it can lead to developing unhealthy habits like seeking comfort and solace in substances that might make us feel better, such as drugs and alcohol.

Studies have shown that people who are happy and engaged at work tend to enjoy life more, they also have better health, stronger relationships and a greater sense of purpose. According to a 2017 Gallup report, engaged employees are more likely to drive innovation and reach their performance objectives. In order to be engaged and happy at work, employees need a sense of purpose, work that is challenging, and feelings of accomplishment, being part of the team and job-security.

Let's keep it real, we all have to work for a living if we want to maintain some level of comfort. Work is important and it is easy to get caught up with day-to-day responsibilities, however, life balance and personal happiness are not tied to earning more money and being successful at work or in business. That's why it is vital to keep in mind the bigger picture—living life to the fullest.

You feel like your boss is making your work-life difficult. Consider the following,

A) Some people like drama and it pours into their professional life.

B) Non-confrontational conversations can be helpful to overcome the situation.

Takeaway: Ideally, people in leadership positions should want to help their teams and others succeed. Before you assume your boss is purposely trying to make your work-life difficult, try to have a conversation with him or her to clear the air, it could be your boss only wants you to excel and thus has a disciplined approach of leading that may come off as rigid. If you are convinced your boss is purposely making your work-life difficult and have proof of this claim, then you could consider reporting it to the human resources department or look for another job. It could end up being the best decision you ever made.

You think a coworker is trying to undermine your hard work. Consider the following,

A) Make sure you can back up your claims.

B) When you do a good job and are recognized for your efforts, it can make others around you insecure.

Takeaway: As a rule of thumb, it is best not to socialize with people that you *know* do not have your best interest at heart. An important statistic noted in the 2017 Gallup report is that nearly one out of five employees are actively disengaged, and these are the people who are sabotaging projects, backstabbing colleagues and creating conflict in the workplace in one way or another. If a coworker is trying to sabotage or undermine your hard work, aim to interact with them only on a need-to-work-with-you basis. If you have a good relationship with your boss and this is affecting your productivity or happiness, you may want to share your experience. Also, distancing yourself from manipulative people is key.

You were fired or laid off. Consider the following,

A) Jobs come and go, you can get another job.

B) There are non-traditional ways of making money these days since the creation of smartphone apps.

Takeaway: Whether you were fired or laid off, look at the situation as a blessing in disguise. Take the knowledge you learned at this job and apply it at the next place you work at. Every experience helps us better ourselves for the future and the next chapter of our life. Earning an income is obviously important to sustain your quality of life. Remember that jobs may come and go, but you still have knowledge and knowledge is power, and if it means that you pursue earning a degree or adding onto the degree(s) you may already have or even relevant certifications in your respective field, you should do it. If it means seeking employment through non-traditional jobs, like a smartphone app, then do it.

Your workload is increasing and it is hindering your productivity. Consider the following,

A) You can reevaluate if this is what you want to do.

B) Open dialogues with your boss about deliverables is a good approach.

Takeaway: It can be a rewarding feeling to know that your boss sees how capable you are at your job, but you must be fair to yourself. If your workload is too overwhelming, it is only fair that you address your concern with your boss and level-set expectations. Designate a meeting when it is convenient for your boss and let him or her know that while you are happy to take on extra work, your current workload is inhibiting your productivity, and perhaps it can be allotted to other teammates who may not be as bogged down with tasks as you are.

You think you deserve a promotion, raise or title-change. Consider the following,

A) You will never know until you ask.

B) Make sure you can prove you actually deserve it.

Takeaway: When people do good work, it certainly warrants recognition, especially in the workplace. People definitely need incentives at work to keep them content and motivated to take on or achieve more. If receiving more pay is tied to more experience, then do what you have to do to demonstrate you deserve the recognition and if that means going back to school or taking classes to further yourself and your career, then by all means, do it. There will always be opportunities in life, you need to either find them or make it happen for you by empowering yourself with more knowledge.

You were referred to do business with a coworker's relative or friend and got ripped off. Consider the following,

A) It is better not to mix your work life with your personal life.

B) You may trust your coworker but you do not know their relative or friend on a personal level.

Takeaway: As wonderful as it may be when a coworker helps you by referring you to a relative or friend of theirs, it is best to leave these two worlds separate. You may have a good relationship with your coworker but the fact is, you do not really know the person they are referring you to. As helpful as it may seem to you, view it from the perspective that your coworker is helping their relative or friend more than they are helping you. In this sour situation, you have learned a valuable lesson in trust and doing your own research. Since you may have to interact with your coworker more frequently than you would like, do not burn the bridge even if it has already caught a bit of fire.

You trusted a coworker with a secret and they told.
Consider the following,

A) Just because you work with someone does not mean you can trust them.

B) Do not confront them or address this situation at work.

Takeaway: In a situation like this, confrontation could only lead to more problems. You must take the higher road and not engage this person. Allow your relationship to fizzle out because work, after all, keeps you very busy. At this point, what your coworker said is simply gossip and unsubstantiated. You have learned a valuable lesson, keep secrets or valued information to yourself or share with people you have trust and confidence in.

You were written up. Consider the following,

A) Sometimes written action must be taken in order to prove a resolution has occurred.

B) Make an active effort to improve or rectify the situation moving forward.

Takeaway: People get written-up for reasons that were a result of their actions or for reasons beyond their control. If you are a hardworking employee and dedicated to your job, one write-up will not negatively affect you. If you were written up as a result of an action you took that proved unfavorable, simply learn from the experience so you do not repeat it and move forward. Do not take this write-up to heart, continue doing the best job you can do and move past it with the highest degree of professionalism.

You were demoted. Consider the following,

A) At least you have a job.

B) Your title does not define you as a person.

Takeaway: You have a job and are earning an income, some people are not as lucky as you. There are people who cannot find work and are unable to pay their bills. Be thankful that even though you do not have the same title and/or job responsibilities, you are employed. Your title at work does not define who you are as a person and it is risky to tie your identity to a title that can be stripped in a heartbeat.

You feel you were short-changed on your severance package. Consider the following,

A) There is more to life than money.

B) There is no harm in asking your employer if they can consider a higher severance.

Takeaway: Do not always count on being offered a severance package you agree with. If you feel you were short-changed, then it is best to remind yourself about all the other perks you may have had while you were employed with this company. Oftentimes, companies are going through financial difficulties themselves and it can be challenging for them to justify a hefty severance package while they have other financial responsibilities or obligations. You can and will find another source of income, in the meantime, be thankful you were offered anything at all.

You do not like your coworkers. Consider the following,

A) Maintain professionalism at all times.

B) You do not have to like your coworkers to accomplish shared tasks.

Takeaway: Getting along with your coworkers can make your job a lot easier. If you do not like one or a few coworkers, that is OK, not all people like each other. However, just because you do not like them does not mean that you cannot maintain a professional demeanor or accomplish shared tasks. Continue to focus on your work. If your relationship with your coworker(s) is interfering with your work, you may want to get some advice from your boss or the human resources or employee relations department.

You did not receive a bonus. Consider the following,

A) Sometimes companies are under financial duress.

B) Be thankful if you have a steady income.

Takeaway: Sometimes, receiving a bonus is not possible, but it does not mean that you will not receive a bonus ever again. If you are not struggling financially, then do not put too much emphasis on this. Even though our livelihoods and quality of life is based on how much money we have, remember that it is not everything. There is more to life than money and certainly more to life than bonuses.

An employee is not meeting your expectations. Consider the following,

A) Always level-set expectations.

B) Open communication between boss and employee is key.

Takeaway: Anytime you begin the process of searching for candidates, it is a good rule of thumb to begin on the right foot by level-setting expectations during the interview process, during the hiring process, during the on-boarding process, and throughout that person's employment at the company. Open, honest communication about achievable deliverables is key to any working relationship.

You are being harassed by a coworker. Consider the following,

A) Tell the human resources or employee relations manager.

B) Depending on the level of harassment, you may have to report the incident to the police.

Takeaway: If you are being harassed in the workplace—physically, verbally, emotionally and/or sexually—it needs to be reported immediately. Companies have teams or departments that are trained to handle these types of situations. Pay a visit to the human resources or employee relations manager. If the harassment escalates to inappropriate behavior like stalking, reporting the incident(s) to the police should be your next step.

You are unemployed and cannot find a job. Consider the following,

A) Clearly define your goal and create daily objectives to achieve it.

B) Consider starting your own business.

Takeaway: There are two ways to view this situation, 1) embrace it and be driven by it, or 2) succumb to it and be angry about it. Being without a job is scary. In fact, anything that derails our routine and comfort is scary. When a person is unable to find a job, their sense of monetary stability is compromised, causing them to become insecure. It is best to never doubt your abilities in moments like this. Sometimes not having a job can be a blessing in disguise because it forces you to think of other options for making money, perhaps options that you would not have considered in the first place, like starting your own business. Take this time to achieve the tasks and dare I say the dreams you did not think you could achieve.

CHAPTER 6

ACADEMIA

"Being ignorant is not so much a shame,
as being unwilling to learn."
–Benjamin Franklin

E ducation is a necessity in life if you want to get ahead, regardless of age. Knowledge is power and human beings have the ability to never stop learning. Every experience in life is an opportunity to learn and grow. Having a solid education can help us prepare for life experiences because by attaining knowledge, we learn new tools to help us deal with our problems or the obstacles we face.

Attending school or any learning-driven institution has its perks. For example, school serves a number of purposes such as building confidence, boosting self-esteem, teaching the importance of discipline and teamwork, and establishing and maintaining friendships—all of which are fundamental social characteristics any successful, productive member of society should possess.

At school, teachers help to guide and prepare pupils for real-life situations by emphasizing the importance of having a daily routine, which is of utmost importance as they're directed, in time, toward the workplace. Additionally, students are provided with access to new ideas and are given the opportunity to learn more about the world through classes that focus on history, culture, geography, language, mathematics and more. Without learning institutions like schools, people would lack the information they need to help themselves succeed and their access to new ideas and knowledgeable people would be limited or simply cut off.

With that being said, an important factor at the forefront of schools is the subject and act of bullying. No matter our age, being made fun of does not feel good. The National Center for Education Statistics revealed that in 2015, more than one out of every five students reported being bullied during the school year.

Though there is no definitive evidence, researchers at Yale School of Medicine have found signs of an apparent connection between bullying, being bullied and suicide in children. School should be a safe-haven, a place where students feel protected and are encouraged to pursue their dreams, not an institution they fear.

Oftentimes, the pressures of succeeding academically or fitting in with friends can play a big role in the decisions and choices we make. No matter how you may feel—sad, angry, stressed and/or depressed—try to rationalize your feelings. You are not alone in how you feel and there are others who have had similar experiences, the goal is to grow from them.

Your grades are below average. Consider the following,

A) Try harder by putting more effort into your work.

B) Talk to your teacher about how you can improve.

Takeaway: Your grades are a reflection of the effort you put into your work. If you put in the effort, then it will be reflected by you earning high grades. If there is a lack of effort when it comes to your schoolwork, then it will be reflected by low grades. The beauty about this situation is you have the power to change it by trying harder. Speak to your teacher(s) and let them know you are serious about their class and earning good grades. Discuss your goals, create a plan together to raise your grades and ask about the possibility of getting extra-credit work. By taking the initiative, your teachers will be more inclined to help you take the extra steps you need to succeed. Every little bit of effort counts.

You feel like you may not get accepted into a university. Consider the following,

A) There are alternatives and options available, like getting a job.

B) You can always attend a community college or technical school.

Takeaway: Years of slacking off at school will catch up to you at some point. However, this does not mean that you have no options. Sometimes by not achieving a goal, we begin to try harder and end up succeeding. Before you jump to any conclusions of not getting accepted, think positively and wait for the official letter. If you did not get accepted into the university of your choice, or any at all, that does not mean you are hopeless. In fact, there is hope. You have many options, including getting a job, and/or attending a community college or technical school, or even reapplying. Figure

AVNI PAREKH

out a plan that will help you achieve your goal. You can do it, but first, you must make that choice.

There is a rumor being spread about you. Consider the following,

A) Do not allow a rumor to ruin your life.

B) Talk to your parents about it.

Takeaway: Rumors are hurtful and can cause more problems than some people realize. When someone is spreading a rumor about you, the best decision you can make is to confide your problem to a trusted adult, like your parents. It is important that the people you love and who love you—your parents and family—are aware of the situation so they can help you. Do not hide what is going on in your life because you think you can handle it or because you are embarrassed. Rumors are not worth hating yourself. Know that you are important and your well-being is important to the people that care about you.

Your SAT and/or ACT scores were not as high as you expected. Consider the following,

A) You can always retake the SAT and/or ACT.

B) Universities and colleges look at more than just test scores, extracurricular activities count too.

Takeaway: Do not be deterred just because your test scores were not what you expected. You can always retake the tests. Plus, your scores account for a percentage of what universities and colleges are looking for. Good grades help because they demonstrate a willingness to learn. Involvement in extracurricular activities

- 62 -

is important as well because it helps to demonstrate your level of commitment to the activity. These institutions are looking for well-rounded students with goals, and being goal-oriented is essential if you seek success in your life.

You were suspended or expelled. Consider the following,

A) It is not cool to cause problems at school.

B) The student, as well as their parents, will be negatively impacted.

Takeaway: When a student is suspended or expelled, it is generally as a result of something they did that goes against school rules. If you were suspended, be grateful the judgment was not worse, and shape up. If you were expelled, you not only make matters difficult for you but you also make matters difficult for your parents who are responsible for managing your education and well-being. As a good rule of thumb, always aim to make informed decisions. Before you act out of impulse, think about how your decision will affect you and others around you.

You are worried because you found out you are pregnant. Consider the following,

A) It is important to let your parents know so they can help you.

B) You have options available to you.

Takeaway: Having a child is a big responsibility that requires a lot of thought, including pre- and post-planning. Regardless of the positive or negative circumstances surrounding your pregnancy, it is important to share the news with your parents or caretakers so they can help guide you through this. You are not alone and have options. It is up to you to make the choice that is right for you, without fear of backlash.

You think a friend may need serious emotional help. Consider the following,

A) A genuine friend will do the best they can to inform the appropriate people.

B) Staying quiet can lead to complex problems.

Takeaway: If a friend is in trouble, tell an adult who can help like a school counselor or even your parents, they will have a better idea of what to do. The act of you telling should not be viewed as you being a snitch, rather a concerned friend looking out for your friend's well-being. Sometimes, staying quiet can lead to complex problems in the future that often have negative results and affect many people.

You are being teased because of your religion or ethnicity. Consider the following,

A) If you are secure with your faith and value your culture, you will be fine.

B) People are not defined by their religion or ethnicity.

Takeaway: Be proud of your ethnic identity and religious background. Be proud of where your family came from and how they got to where they are now. Do not allow anyone to break your faith or impact your cultural pride. If you are secure with your faith and value your culture, then you will find the strength to overcome the teasing. There is no right or wrong religion and no supreme race or ethnic group. We are all human beings and should not be defined by the religion we practice or judged because of the part of the world we come from.

You are being teased because of how you look.
Consider the following,

A) Insecure people make fun of others to boost their own self-esteem.

B) You are special, plain and simple.

Takeaway: Be proud of who you are. Do not let the insecurities of other people have the power to bring you down. Physical appearance does not define you as a person, and those people who think their looks define them are mistaken about what life is about. Beauty is comprised of more than just physical appearance, it encompasses inner-beauty as well. True beauty is about who you are on the inside. You are beautiful because you possess traits that are unique to you and only you.

You are being teased because of your sexual orientation.
Consider the following,

A) Have the courage to move forward living your life—it is your life and no one else's.

B) Some people tend to criticize and judge people and concepts they do not understand.

Takeaway: Be happy and confident in who you are as a person. Some people make fun of others because they are not happy with their own lives or they simply do not understand how to expand their minds. Just because someone does not understand you or your choice to love who you love, does not mean there is anything wrong with you. If you have good intentions, then there is truly nothing to worry about. Surround yourself with people who support and love you for who you are and the wonderful qualities that make you unique.

You are being bullied online and/or in person. Consider the following,

A) Bullies, including cyber-bullies, think they have power by hurting others.

B) Confide to a person—you trust—who can help you.

Takeaway: Do not allow negative, spiteful people to impact your sense of self-worth and your overall happiness. Bullies are people who suffer from emotional issues. When people blatantly try to demoralize others, it is because of their own insecurity issues. If a select group of people are tormenting you, instead of hiding the fact that you are being bullied relentlessly, tell your parents or someone you trust who has the ability to help. If you are being bullied online, you must remember that these people do not really know you. Be strong and do not allow anyone to make you feel less than what you are: special.

You are being peer-pressured to do something you would not ordinarily do. Consider the following,

A) Do not succumb to peer-pressure.

B) It is better to be a leader than a follower.

Takeaway: If someone is pressuring you to do something that you know is not ethical or simply not right for you and your life, it is OK to say "no." You do not have to succumb to peer-pressure just because everybody is doing it. It is cooler to make informed decisions rather than follow the crowd. Before making a snap decision, think about the consequences of your actions. Be a leader, not a follower. Stand by your decision and do not be afraid to say "no."

You failed a class. Consider the following,

A) You owe it to yourself to aim for higher goals.

B) If you try harder, you will be able to pass.

Takeaway: The feeling of failing a class or even an entire grade can be devastating but the good news is that it is not the end of the world. Failing a class or being set back a grade does not mean you are a failure. The best way to approach this situation is to figure out the factors that contributed to this outcome and then not to repeat them moving forward. If you try harder, then you will pass—that is a guarantee. You owe it to yourself to aim for higher goals and to hold yourself accountable for achieving those goals.

You cannot financially keep up with your friends. Consider the following,

A) Being able to afford the newest and coolest gadgets and clothes will not bring you happiness.

B) Genuine friends will like you for who you are on the inside and not for your possessions.

Takeaway: When you are not as well-off or privileged as your friends or the people you surround yourself with, it can elicit feelings of insecurity or inferiority. Being able to afford the latest and greatest gadgets or clothes will not bring you happiness. Good and genuine friends will keep their company with you because of how you make them feel and who you are as a person, and not because of how much money you have or your possessions.

You want to commit suicide. Consider the following,

A) Your life is worth living.

B) You are more special than you realize or give yourself credit for.

Takeaway: Do not ever think that your life is not worth living. There are people around you—family, friends and strangers alike—who genuinely care about you and want to see the best for you. They will do anything in their power to protect you, so know that you are not alone nor are you a burden to anyone. When you make a brash decision like taking your life, you not only hurt the people around you but you place them in an internal state of torment, the very feeling you are trying to escape. Learn to love yourself because you are special and there is no one else like you on this planet.

CHAPTER 7

——•——◦——•——

DRIVING

*"For every minute you remain angry, you give
up sixty seconds of peace of mind."*
– **Ralph Waldo Emerson**

I n addition to spending a lot of time at work and school, we also spend a lot of time in our vehicles, driving from place to place. Just like the comfort and security a home provides, a car can also provide a sense of security. Driving is a privilege, not a right, so it is really important to make wise and informed decisions when driving or operating a motor vehicle.

There are numerous obstacles and many distractions we can face on the road and when they threaten our security, our ability to make informed decisions can be inhibited. Say you are driving to work and someone is tailgating you and five minutes later someone flicks you off, wouldn't you be ticked off? What if the person driving in front of you or next to you is texting? The National Highway Traffic Safety Administration reported in

2015, nearly one in five crashes where someone was injured was due to distracted drivers.

According to a study published in the Journal of Experimental Psychology: Applied, people made more errors while driving when talking on a cell phone as opposed to talking with another passenger. In fact, additional research from another study published in Human Factors shows that the impairments associated with cell phone usage while driving may be as great as those commonly observed by intoxicated drivers with a blood-alcohol level of .08— the legal limit in the United States. The research even indicates that hands-free, voice-activated calls can be just as distracting as handheld cell phone conversations.

Every driver should be mindful of the other drivers around them. Your actions affect them and their actions affect you. Cars are not toys, they are a means for transportation. When they are not used carefully, they can act as weapons, and sometimes we do not get a second chance or a do-over.

Drivers should, a) be sober and alert, b) remain calm and focused, and c) act responsibly and make the best choices while driving despite the obstacles that may arise along the way. A primary example of exerting good decision making is being prepared not to drive if you decide to drink, it's that simple.

If we, as a society, could think of the road as a communal space we all share, instead of a piece of property we own, then we may be able to work together as opposed to against each other. The reason traffic is supposed to flow is because drivers are supposed to go with the flow.

A driver cut you off. Consider the following,

A) Safety on the road should be every driver's main concern.

B) Many people are poor drivers.

Takeaway: It is very easy to get agitated when someone cuts you off in traffic or if someone is driving recklessly. Your safety and the safety of others around you should be your primary concern. Be mindful that your actions on the road do not put anyone in danger. If there is a reckless or careless driver near you, do your best to get as far away from that person as soon as possible. Obey the speed signs and remain cautious. The road is a dangerous place, so please drive carefully.

A driver stuck their middle finger at you. Consider the following,

A) People have bad days and often take it out on others around them.

B) Be mindful that your actions have not caused the other driver to react that way.

Takeaway: When most people get on the road, their main mission is getting from point A to point B, which can sometimes affect other drivers because they are only focusing on their end destination and not the road. Do not get upset if a driver throws their middle finger up at you, they could just be having a bad day and taking it out on you. You have the power to exert self-control by not engaging this person. But, if for some reason, you accidentally cut them off, make sure you do not provoke any further response that could cause harm to you, them or other innocent people around you.

You are being tailgated or angrily honked at by a driver exhibiting road-rage. Consider the following,

A) Tailgaters are a threat to everyone's safety on the road.

B) Remain calm.

Takeaway: Always consider your safety on the road, as well as others around you. Do not provoke or instigate aggressive drivers. If you observe the person behind you driving very close to your car, the best and safest option would be to stay calm and change lanes, allowing this person to pass. It will not help matters if you become upset and decide to purposely press on your brakes. This could probably agitate the person behind you further and cause them to lash out. If the person continues to follow you while displaying aggressive behavior, try to remain calm and call 9-1-1 immediately.

A driver is weaving in and out of traffic. Consider the following,

A) Stay far away from erratic drivers.

B) Call the police.

Takeaway: All drivers must be alert and sober when they make the choice to drive. It is also important to mention that by driving under the influence of mind-altering substances like drugs and alcohol, irresponsible drivers not only endanger themselves but they endanger the lives of innocent people around them. When you observe someone driving erratically, your main concern should be to stay far away. If it is clear that the driver may be impaired or distracted for whatever reason, the best decision to make would be to call the police to notify them of this driver who poses a threat to other drivers on the road.

A driver is texting. Consider the following,

A) Every driver's attention should be focused on the road.

B) If a driver is texting while driving, then their focus is *not* on the road.

Takeaway: Reading and responding to text messages while driving is not acceptable. The only object that should be in a person's hand while driving is the steering wheel. Do not let the urgency of knowing what is on someone's mind distract you from driving safely. In this situation, do yourself a big favor and carefully move into another lane when the opportunity arises. You do not want to take a chance driving near or next to someone whose focus is clearly shifted from safety on the road.

A driver next to you is blasting their music. Consider the following,

A) You can change lanes and move away.

B) You can put your windows up.

Takeaway: Every driver has the right to blast their music. This person is probably trying to enjoy their drive as much as you may be. If they are not tailgating you, driving erratically or anything that can be considered dangerous, then they are not hurting anyone. You could be a bit stressed and this is why the loud music could be bothering you. Please stay calm and simply put your windows up if it is bothering you that much. When the time and opportunity presents itself, change lanes and move away.

You were pulled over for speeding and/or drag-racing. Consider the following,

A) You are putting yourself and other drivers at risk.

B) It is against the law.

Takeaway: Though speeding and drag-racing may give you a thrill, both acts are against the law. These laws are in place not to hinder your fun but to keep you and other drivers safe. Speeding and drag-racing are reckless acts that can have far greater consequences than the fun they are built up to be.

A motorcyclist is driving erratically. Consider the following,

A) It is never wise to play around on the road.

B) Every vehicle, including a motorcycle, is a weapon.

Takeaway: All vehicles are deadly weapons and should be driven with caution. It is not impressive to watch reckless motorcyclists endanger innocent drivers around them. Driving erratically and/or doing wheelies on the road or any area that is designated for pedestrians and drivers is unacceptable. The road is not the place for games. Move aside and keep your distance until this person or group of people pass you by.

Your car got towed. Consider the following,

A) Be mindful that you are not parking in a tow-away zone.

B) Make arrangements to get your car back.

Takeaway: It is a good rule of thumb to be aware of your surroundings. When parking your car, make sure you are not parking in a restricted or tow-away zone. If your car was towed, you have no other choice but to go through the motions and get your car back. Try not to be too frustrated because it will not help the situation and will only stress you out more.

A bicyclist is blocking your lane. Consider the following,

A) Bicyclists have just as much right on the road as drivers do.

B) Do not get frustrated.

Takeaway: Bicyclists have every right to cycle on the road and are subject to the same traffic laws as motorists. The speed of a bike certainly cannot compare to the speed of a car and the force of a car striking a bike is even more powerful than if it were to hit another car. Though it can be frustrating to get stuck behind someone riding their bike on the road, you must remain calm and wait for the chance to switch lanes.

You are stuck in a traffic jam. Consider the following,

A) Just accept it.

B) Find something to do, like checking your emails while your car is stationary or listening to music.

Takeaway: Depending on the nature of the traffic jam, you may get going sooner rather than later or you could be stuck for a few hours. If you are not moving anywhere anytime soon and might be stuck for a long period of time, try to be productive. For instance, check your email, do some research, or make some important phone calls. Try to get tasks accomplished while you are stuck, this way you do not waste time. Getting upset is not going to do you any good. It would be better to accept the situation for what it is and make the best of it.

You got into an accident. Consider the following,

A) Always wear your seatbelt.

B) Cars can always be replaced, human life cannot.

Takeaway: When driving, a person's first priority should be safety. When you get into a car, whether you are in the front seat or the back seat, you must wear your seatbelt. The seatbelt is a safety mechanism designed to protect you. Getting into an accident or a fender bender is aggravating but cars and car parts can always be replaced, your life and/or the lives of others, however, cannot. Remember to stay calm, regardless of who is at fault. A rude disposition will not get you anywhere but a kind disposition will. Take the appropriate steps to resolve this situation. Be thankful that the outcome was not worse.

You received a traffic ticket. Consider the following,

A) It happens to just about everyone.

B) Be mindful of the law while driving on the road.

Takeaway: Getting a traffic ticket is a moment that many people will experience at some point in their lives. This is just an indicator to be mindful of everything you do while driving. There is no point in being rude to the officer. If you are not sure what you did, be polite in how you ask. Receiving a ticket is not really a big deal. There are several options you can choose from to resolve this.

Your car broke down on the road. Consider the following,

A) Put your hazard lights on immediately.

B) Move to a safe spot, if possible.

Takeaway: If your car broke down on the road, put your car's hazard lights on to indicate to others around you that something is wrong. If by chance you are able to pull your car to the median, then do so. Call road-side assistance immediately or someone you can rely on to help you. Also, as much as you may want to get out of your car, it could be a better decision to stay inside of your car. The road, just like life, is unpredictable. Minimizing any danger that could come to you should be a priority.

You were indicating for a parking space and another driver took it. Consider the following,

A) Be careful, confrontations could lead to disaster.

B) People who have no regard for what is acceptable societal behavior can be dangerous.

Takeaway: Even though you are frustrated, it could be a wise decision to just let it be and find another spot, even if it took you a while to find an available space. Confronting a person who did not have regard for your claim to the parking space will do you no good. People who demonstrate a lack of care can be unpredictable and in some cases, dangerous. Save your energy for what really matters. At the end of the day, it is just a parking space and has no value to your life and overall well-being.

CHAPTER 8

FLYING

*"Man must rise above the Earth—to the top of the
atmosphere and beyond—for only thus will he fully
understand the world in which he lives."*
–Socrates

The airline industry has changed immensely over the last 100
years, and as time goes on and our understanding of technology
advances, more changes will continue to take place.

For some, flying can be an enjoyable experience and for others,
it can be a nightmare. There are many factors that can go wrong
when airplanes and airports are concerned, everything from
mechanical issues to technical issues to personal issues, but one
thing is for sure, no two flights are ever the same.

Most people are unaware that airplane cabins aren't an optimal
environment to foster good health. Though airplanes are designed
to get us from place to place in a quicker amount of time as

opposed to using other methods of transportation, they still pose risks to our respiratory and circulatory systems, like dehydration, breathing problems and lung damage, the spread of communicable diseases, and developing conditions like leg clots and even cancer. In fact, compelling evidence published in JAMA Dermatology shows that pilots and cabin crew have an increased incidence of melanoma. Other studies have indicated that female flight attendants are five times more likely to develop breast cancer than the general population.

Aside from that, more than eight million people fly on a plane daily, according to the International Air Transportation Association. Could you imagine how many frustrated passengers there could be worldwide? What if you are on an airplane and the flight attendant was rude, or the passenger next to you was snoring? When nothing seems to be going right and multiple people, all with different personalities and temperaments, are trapped in an enclosed space for any given amount of time, tensions can rise quickly.

To minimize the chance of conflicts, try to anticipate some of your needs ahead of time so you can be prepared when or if it happens. For example, if you have an inclination that you may not like their snacks, then bring your own. If you get cold easily, then bring a blanket.

Every passenger wants to leave their flight satisfied and in order to do so, it is a good idea to practice patience and be diplomatic about how you approach the one or many obstacles you may encounter during your flight.

A flight attendant is being rude. Consider the following,

A) Maybe he or she is having a bad day.

B) Speak to another flight attendant.

Takeaway: Being stuck in close quarters with a bunch of strangers is not exactly fun, especially if some people are not very pleasant to be around. Flight attendants deal with hundreds of people on a frequent basis. They often have to deal with very rude passengers and sometimes that can take a toll on their outlook that day. Do your best not to take their rude response or demeanor personally, rather engage another flight attendant who could be of more help to you. If their rudeness comes off as prejudice, then take the appropriate steps to report or document that attendant's behavior.

The passenger seated next to you is being rude. Consider the following,

A) Not all people are courteous and respectful.

B) Discretely ask the flight attendant to move to another available seat.

Takeaway: Being seated next to someone unpleasant can have a negative effect on your sky-high voyage. Have compassion for people who are outwardly rude. Do not allow someone's negative attitude to affect the way you carry yourself. Find a moment when you can discretely speak to a flight attendant and explain the situation. You are not trying to make a scene; you would just like to find an empty seat where you can relocate to enjoy the rest of your flight. Flight attendants are often very understanding and want to be of help.

The passenger seated next to you will not stop talking to you. Consider the following,

A) Some people are very talkative.

B) Approach the situation with kindness.

Takeaway: Some people are very chatty and will make conversation with just about anyone. There is nothing wrong with this and oftentimes, this is how friends are made. If this person's overly chattiness is getting on your nerves, be kind and simply let the person know that although you would love to chat, you prefer to rest for the moment. You can be kind without being rude and creating conflict.

A passenger is snoring loudly. Consider the following,

A) Snoring cannot always be controlled.

B) Try to be understanding.

Takeaway: Do not disturb someone if you do not have to. Snoring is difficult to control and can be a result of sleep disorders, nasal issues, lack of sleep, among other reasons. If the snoring is getting on your nerves, then use earplugs or earphones to drown out the noise. If you did not pack either, then discreetly ask a flight attendant if there are any unoccupied seats so that you could relocate for the duration of your flight, if that helps.

A passenger's baby will not stop crying. Consider the following,

A) Babies cry and it is not intentional.

B)   It is probably ten times more frustrating for the parent(s).

Takeaway: It can be very irritating when babies will not stop crying. Please remember that neither the parent nor the child is purposely trying to annoy you. It is probably very frustrating for the parent(s) as well. Think about it, not being able to help your baby is frustrating and being on a flight with strangers who do not know your situation can make it even more difficult. If you have earphones, make use of them. Have compassion for the situation, you could be in that situation one day yourself.

A passenger is playing their music or movie loudly. Consider the following,

A)   Some people are not mindful of their actions and others are inconsiderate.

B)   We all seek out entertaining distractions to offset long or boring flights.

Takeaway: Many people prepare for long and/or boring flights by packing electronic gadgets like iPods and iPads to serve as distractions. Ideally, headphones or earphones get packed too. The folks you see with these gadgets are often in their own bubble, minding their business. Being able to decipher if a person is intentionally doing something to annoy you is vital to shrugging off common annoyances. If the passenger's music or movie is obnoxiously loud, rest assured that flight attendants will mention it.

Your flight was delayed or got diverted. Consider the following,

A)   Delays happen all the time.

B) Find something productive or worthwhile to do.

Takeaway: Flights get delayed and/or diverted all the time, for reasons known and unknown. Flying poses risks just like anything in life. It would be worse if you were in the air and encountered a problem, so be thankful that the airline is looking out for your well-being by delaying or diverting your flight. If you have a chance to be productive, then take the opportunity. It could also be a great opportunity to catch up on some much-needed rest. You will end up at your destination at some point, just be patient, calm and polite.

You missed your flight. Consider the following,

A) There is nothing you can do but wait for the next flight.

B) You *can* control your emotions.

Takeaway: If you missed your flight, there is nothing you can do besides wait for the next available flight. You are stuck in the situation until you reach your destination and then you can forget the whole incident ever happened. Getting upset is not going to do you any good nor is it going to help you which is why it would be best to control your emotions. Unfortunately, people miss flights on a daily basis.

Your carry-on luggage needs to be checked. Consider the following,

A) If you have to check your luggage, then do it.

B) Do not kick up a fuss.

Takeaway: As frustrating as it may be to check the luggage you intended to carry with you, you must accept it and check your luggage because you will not be allowed on the flight without doing so. Kicking up a fuss will only delay you, and in some cases, could delay the flight from departing on time because your frustration may come off as hostility which leads to the thought of you potentially posing a risk and as you may know, nobody wants to deal with a liability.

Your luggage and/or belongings were lost or stolen. Consider the following,

A) Take the appropriate steps to report the situation.

B) Luckily, clothes and other material possessions can be replaced.

Takeaway: When traveling, it is a good idea to pack items that you do not have an emotional attachment to. If your bags were lost, the airline will try to locate it and send it back to you. In cases where your luggage or belongings were stolen, you can take the appropriate measures to report it and then replace those items yourself.

A passenger is rushing to disembark the plane. Consider the following,

A) Some people lack patience or they are rushing for a connecting flight.

B) The plane's door must be open for passengers to be able to disembark.

Takeaway: It can be easy to understand how people can become restless during and after a flight. Some people are also rushing to catch connecting flights which can cause them to become extremely anxious and impatient. Try to keep that in mind and not get too agitated by this passenger's behavior and/or commentary. As soon as the plane's door is opened, everyone will have their chance to disembark the plane.

The passenger sitting next to you smells bad.
Consider the following,

A) Politely ask the flight attendant if you can move.

B) You may have no other choice but to endure it.

Takeaway: No one favors being stuck next to a stranger, for any length of time, especially while they are emitting an unpleasant odor. Truth be told, bad smells can be very sickening for some people. If this applies to you, discretely ask the flight attendant if you could move to an empty seat and explain the reason for your request. If you are unable to move, then spray some perfume or cologne but know that this is frowned upon as some people may have sensitivities to bottled-scents. If you do not have either on hand, then you may have to suck it up and bear it. Sometimes, people are not aware of their bad body odor, so try to be polite and understanding.

You were kicked off the flight for unruly behavior.
Consider the following,

A) Every decision we make has a consequence, whether it be positive or negative.

B) Compose yourself while at the airport and on board the plane.

Takeaway: You are not in a fraternity- or sorority-house, please grow up. Every decision we make and every action we take has consequences and/or a reaction. Conduct yourself with decorum and dignity when at the airport and while on board, and anywhere for that matter. Exhibiting unruly behavior at the airport not only affects you, it affects the other passengers too.

The passenger seated in front of you keeps pushing their seat back. Consider the following,

A) People can become restless and fidgety.

B) Politely ask the passenger if they would stop.

Takeaway: Passengers can become restless when on board, and that can translate into fidgety movements while seated. The passenger seated in front of you may not be aware that you are being inconvenienced. If you feel like you need to tell them, then tap them gently and politely explain how the seat's rocking is affecting your comfort.

You were sexually harassed or groped by a passenger on the plane. Consider the following,

A) Be aware of your surroundings, which includes being aware of the people around you.

B) Notify a flight attendant the moment you feel uncomfortable.

Takeaway: No matter where you are, it is a good idea to be aware and alert of your surroundings and the people around you. If you are being sexually harassed by a passenger on the plane, do not remain silent, tell them to stop and to leave you alone. Do not be afraid to inform a flight attendant if the situation escalates and especially if your rights have been violated through inappropriate touching or fondling, that is called sexual assault and offenders should be held accountable. Report the incident immediately.

CHAPTER 9

TRAGEDY

*"One word frees us of all the weight
and pain in life. That word is love."*
—Sophocles

Why do bad things happen to good people? Why do good people have to suffer for the wrongdoings of one or a few bad seeds? Why are people becoming so careless? What happened to caring about one another? How did humanity get to a point where mass shootings and acts of terrorism occur on a weekly basis? The questions seem endless and it seems like everywhere we turn, something tragic has taken place.

Tragedy is defined as an event that causes great suffering, destruction and distress. Trauma is defined as a deeply distressing or disturbing experience and is often the result of an event, series of events or set of circumstances experienced by an individual— physically or emotionally—that is perceived as harmful or threatening to their well-being. Trauma can have lasting adverse effects and can take a serious emotional toll on those involved, even if the event did not cause physical damage. Regardless of its source, emotional trauma encompasses three common elements, 1) the event was unexpected, 2) the person was unprepared, and 3) there was nothing the person could do to prevent the event from happening. Therefore, it is not the event itself that determines if trauma will arise. Rather, it's the individual's personal experience of the event that determines if they will be traumatized.

Tragedies occur in all forms and are unpredictable in nature. In fact, most people will experience at least one tragic event in their lifetime. For example, how do you process your perception of life and cope with reality when a loved one commits suicide? Did you know that in 2015, more than 44,000 suicides were reported, ranking suicide as the tenth leading cause of death for Americans as stated by the American Foundation for Suicide Prevention? That means, in that year, someone died by suicide every 13.7 minutes. How about when a loved one was killed by an impaired driver? The National Highway Traffic Safety Administration states that every day, almost 30 people in the United States die in motor vehicle crashes that involve an alcohol-impaired driver, which amounts to one death about every 50 minutes.

According to USA Today's Behind the Bloodshed presentation, 77 percent of mass killings involve a gun, and nearly three out of four guns involved were handguns. The Mass Shooting Tracker reports 477 mass shootings in the United States in 2016, resulting in 604 deaths and wounding 1,783 others.

We are surrounded by tragedy and although nothing can be said or done to turn back the hands of time, we all have the ability to rise above the negative experiences we may encounter in life. In order to achieve this, we must adopt a different perspective about how we view the situation and be grateful for what we have. The other component to this is taking action by using your mind to create a positive change in the world.

A loved one died unexpectedly. Consider the following,

A) Sometimes, there are no logical reasons to explain the tragedies that happen in life.

B) It is OK to feel anger, frustration and sadness.

Takeaway: When a loved one dies unexpectedly, a person's emotions and thoughts will go from one extreme to the other. Making sense of the situation will be difficult and we may doubt our ability to move forward without our loved one present in our life. After experiencing a significant loss, a person may feel grief and pain. Both feelings are normal aspects of coping with death. However, it is important to understand that the grieving process takes time and everyone deals with loss differently and heals at their own pace, and that is OK. Cherish every moment you spend with your loved ones. At some point in life, moments become memories and can be all we have to hold on to.

You are involved in a lengthy and/or messy legal battle. Consider the following,

A) It is better to seek justice lawfully then take matters into your own hands.

B) Remain level-headed.

Takeaway: Money, possessions, reputation and/or other assets of value, like children, are often the cause of contention between feuding people. It is sad when problems cannot be solved amicably. The system is not perfect, but it is better to seek justice lawfully then to take matters into your own hands. Life cannot be controlled, which is why it is important to remain level-headed in situations that can cause your blood pressure to rise.

You were raped or molested. Consider the following,

A)   It is not your fault and you are not to blame.

B)   Have strength and do not allow this experience to ruin your life.

Takeaway: In life, we are bound to go through experiences that may shatter our hopes and/or our will to live. If you were raped or molested, it is important that you know you are *not* to blame. Regardless of the factors surrounding the situation, this is not your fault and no one has the right to take advantage of you. You will experience a range of emotions ranging from shame to anger to sadness, and this is OK. Be strong and do not allow this experience to ruin your life. You are in control of your life and can move past traumatic experiences in due time.

A loved one was paralyzed. Consider the following,

A)   At least you will be able to see them and be with them.

B)   They will need your support now more than ever.

Takeaway: Dealing with a loved one's paralysis can be devastating. Your loved one's quality of life will drastically change and so will the lives of the people closest to them. If rehabilitation can help them regain some sort of normalcy then encourage them as much as possible even though it will be physically painful and emotionally draining. If there is nothing that can be done to improve their condition, be there to love and support them as much as possible. Additionally, if you want to ensure you get the medical care you would want in a situation like or similar to this, it is strongly recommended to document your health care wishes *before* a health care crisis occurs.

You survived a horrific, life-changing event. Consider the following,

A) Be thankful for the gift of life.

B) Use your experience to help others.

Takeaway: Life is unpredictable, regardless of how much we try to plan. Our mortality is more fragile than we think and is often furthest from our mind. If you survived a horrific, life-changing event, be thankful you are still alive. Though the healing process may take long, there is nothing wrong in grieving, and if you need a good cry, then you need a good cry. Try to use your experience to help others who might be going through a similar situation. Be the light in someone's dark tunnel.

You or a loved one were diagnosed with a terminal condition. Consider the following,

A) Life should be lived to the fullest.

B) Treasure each moment you share with your loved ones.

Takeaway: Being diagnosed with a terminal condition is heartbreaking, to say the least. If you were diagnosed with a terminal condition, do your best to make the most of every waking day and explore your end-of-life care options, like electing hospice. Oftentimes, situations like this can be more difficult for loved ones to understand than the person actually living with the condition(s). Watching a loved one suffer from an illness that will eventually kill them can be unbearable. Express your love as often as possible and do whatever you can to help ease their pain, whether it is physical or emotional. Make your loved one feel as special as possible, and make the best of the time you have left with them.

A loved one committed suicide. Consider the following,

A) No amount of rationalizing will help you understand why they did it.

B) Celebrate their life and what made them special.

Takeaway: Some people are very unhappy. It could be unhappiness that has followed them for a lifetime or for a small chapter of their life. No matter how low we feel, life *is* worth living. When a loved one takes their life, the people around them are faced with trying to understand why they did it. Ultimately you will never know what they were thinking when they decided to make that life-ending choice, even if you have a note. We must cherish the time we have with the people we care about because life can change in an instant. Additionally, if you know a loved one suffers from depression, then do what you can to get them the help they need to manage this condition.

A loved one is suffering from a mentally or physically debilitating disease. Consider the following,

A) Your support and love are crucial to their longevity.

B) Do your best to get them the compassionate care they need.

Takeaway: It is difficult to watch your loved one's health decline especially if they are suffering from a mentally or physically debilitating disease. Oftentimes, in situations like this, it is best to get your loved one the care they need to remain comfortable as their disease progresses. Explore options like palliative care or nursing care at home. Your support and love are crucial to their longevity at this sensitive time in their life.

You were pregnant and had a miscarriage. Consider the following,

A) Carrying a pregnancy to full term is not as easy as most may think.

B) Though you may have lost hope, keep trying until you succeed.

Takeaway: Bringing a new life into the world is a gift and a tremendous responsibility. Carrying a viable pregnancy to full term is not as easy as most may think, and the chances for developing complications increase as women get older, that is simply reality. If you were pregnant and suffered a miscarriage, do not lose hope. If your goal is to have a baby, keep trying until you succeed and that includes exploring other options and alternatives to conceiving.

You caused an accident where a person or many people died. Consider the following,

A) The impact this situation will have on you and many others will be life-changing.

B) Take responsibility for your actions.

Takeaway: Death is never an easy event to get over, especially if it was a result of your actions. A situation like this is devastating for all parties involved and affects several more people in the process. The first step is to realize the gravity of your actions and take responsibility for them. Asking for forgiveness from the people who were emotionally impacted as a result can be helpful, but be mindful that forgiveness from others may not come as quickly or never at all. Most importantly, if you are truly remorseful, then forgiving yourself will help as you begin to heal and, if applicable, making wiser decisions to help you avoid conflict is advised.

You were a victim of police brutality. Consider the following,

A) There is no justification for the maltreatment innocent people suffer at the hands of people working in law enforcement.

B) If police were given yearly, mandatory psychological evaluations, we might avoid these situations.

Takeaway: Too often we are hearing and seeing stories about police brutality across the nation. As a citizen, it is troubling to see people being treated poorly, beaten and/or killed by people working in law enforcement whose task is to serve and protect—especially if the situation appears to be unprovoked or unsubstantiated. There is no justification for the maltreatment innocent people suffer at the hands of people working in law enforcement. If police officers and other law enforcement professionals were given yearly, mandatory psychological evaluations, we might be able to minimize and/or avoid these situations. In this type of situation, it is best to seek the guidance of legal counsel, sooner rather than later.

You or a loved one is addicted to drugs and/or alcohol. Consider the following,

A) Alcohol and various other drugs are a poison to the body and can be deadly.

B) Any substance that alters a person's judgment is a hindrance to their well-being.

Takeaway: Doing anything in excess is never a good idea. When a person lives with an addiction, they are not the only ones who suffer, the people around them suffer as well. If you have reached a point where functioning as a contributing member of society is not working, you definitely need to get help, especially for your health and overall well-being. If you notice that your loved one is suffering from an addiction, you should do everything in your power to get them the help and tools they need to overcome this disease. Do not enable unhealthy and dangerous habits.

You are taking care of a chronically ill parent, spouse or child. Consider the following,

A) Though it is tough and draining, you are your loved one's best advocate.

B) Make sure to set aside time for yourself to unwind and enjoy life.

Takeaway: Being a caregiver to a chronically ill parent, spouse or child is emotionally and physically draining. As a caregiver, you are your loved one's best advocate. By being in this role, you also assume the responsibilities of making important decisions regarding their health and well-being. Therefore, it is important to do as much research as possible about the condition or disease so you can better support their needs, including finding organizations that will help them or services they may be entitled to or qualify for. Additionally, it is vital for every caregiver to make time for his or her self and if additional support is needed, then explore the options available.

You think you have ruined your life. Consider the following,

A) You have the power to change your life for the better.

B) In order to change your life, you must actively change your habits and behavior.

Takeaway: Sometimes we get accustomed to making poor choices in life because we lack the knowledge or foresight to understand how these choices can impact us in the present moment as well as the future. Every decision we make has an outcome that sets off a chain reaction of other events that can affect us emotionally, physically and/or financially. If you think you have ruined your life, then know you have the power to change it. The first step is acknowledging the patterns and behaviors you have been accustomed to in the past. The second step is to make an active effort not to repeat them. The moment you begin to change the habits that led you down this path, including staying away from people who are negative influences in your life, is the very moment your life begins to change.

You or a loved one suffer from obesity. Consider the following,

A) Obesity can be treated.

B) There is a deeper issue at stake when people overeat.

Takeaway: Developing good habits is essential in life, no matter what. Establishing a nutritious diet is vital to sustaining optimal health, which should be a priority for everyone. The purpose of eating food is to help the body function. Eating poorly, combined with overeating can affect a person's mind and body, resulting in damaging outcomes. When people overeat, there is a deeper emotional issue at stake. Overeating is not a solution to coping with overwhelming emotions. If you are considered obese, aim to make changes to your diet and seek guidance from a nutritionist, dietician, life coach or someone in a position to help you overcome your emotions and your habit of poor eating. If a loved one is suffering from obesity, get them the tools and resources to help him or her overcome this problem.

CHAPTER 10

PUBLIC PLACES

"The world is a dangerous place to live;
not because of the people who are evil, but because
of the people who don't do anything about it."
–Albert Einstein

The experiences and interactions we have in public with strangers can have a profound effect on our demeanor and can impact how we interact with others around us. In today's society, it seems like people simply cannot control their emotions. They seem to lose their cool easily and take out their frustrations on the people around them when moments they experience do not go the way they expected.

For instance, what do you do when the waiter who served you was rude for no reason, or what happens when someone is invading your personal space? How do you deal with nonsensical experiences that do not really matter in the grand scheme of life?

Empirical evidence suggests that the effect of negative social interactions can be far more harmful than social support is helpful and may have more of a detrimental impact on psychological well-being than positive interactions. As a matter of fact, an especially interesting 2016 study published in the Journal of Personality and Social Psychology proposes that social rejection is linked to aggression, in large part because being rejected damages a person's mood which leads to the psychological need to repair it through the release of retaliatory aggression which studies showed produces a positive effect on the mind, similar to a mirage, that helps to mend their bruised ego. These particular findings are fascinating because they tie aggression's rewarding nature as an incentive for rejected individuals' violent tendencies. However, more research on the implication of negative social interactions must be studied further.

Developing and maintaining self-control is very important. Self-control is what helps us regulate our emotions and impulses, thus enabling us to behave in a manner that is socially acceptable. In fact, a 2013 study published in the Journal of Personality has linked self-control to life satisfaction and long-term happiness. Basically indicating, the better we become at managing conflicting emotions, the better equipped we are at leading an emotionally fulfilling life.

More often than not, people lose sight of what is really important because everyday experiences or 'little things' get in the way of reality. Reality is, knowing that life is too short to dwell on mundane experiences that have no way of bettering the mind and the human spirit. Life is so precious, and we only get one chance— the present moment—to make a difference.

You are receiving poor service. Consider the following,

A) Sometimes, restaurants or retail shops are low-staffed, try to be understanding and maintain your composure.

B) Speak to a manager, write a letter to the establishment or place an online review about your experience.

Takeaway: Good service is essential if a restaurant or retail shop wants to succeed and have returning customers. If you are experiencing poor service as a result of the establishment being low-staffed, then try to be patient. If the poor service seems to be blatant and it is affecting your experience, you can always talk to a manager to voice your concern(s) or you can write a letter to their headquarters or even place an online review.

A stranger is being rude to you for no reason. Consider the following,

A) Some people have abrasive personalities.

B) Do not take it personally.

Takeaway: Sometimes people can be jerks for no reason and negative energy can certainly affect your mood. As a matter of fact, moods—negative and positive—can be contagious, this process is called emotional contagion and studies have shown that it is indeed very real. Instead of allowing this person's bad mood to ruin your day, be thankful that you are able to manage your emotions in public without it interfering in how you interact with others, unlike this person.

**You got into a heated argument or fight with a stranger.
Consider the following,**

A) People have a right to be able to express and share their opinions.

B) Do not allow anger to impact how you carry yourself.

Takeaway: If you are disagreeing with a stranger, agree to disagree and walk away. Do not allow anger to impact how you carry yourself. People have a right to express and share their opinions without persecution. As long as these opinions are not extremist in nature and do not allude to causing physical harm to others, it would be best to shrug it off and not take it personally. A stranger's personal opinion should not carry much weight in your life unless they are being considered for election.

Someone is invading your personal space. Consider the following,

A) Just breathe and do not get upset.

B) Move if there is space.

Takeaway: Nothing is more aggravating than someone invading your personal space. You must remember that while you understand the boundary of giving personal space, others may not. Do not get agitated to the point where you lose your cool. If there is space around you, move a little. If the person moves closer, then you may be out of luck and might have to bear it for the moment. If you can feel them breathing, then you may want to say something in a non-confrontational tone.

There is no accommodation for your disability.
Consider the following,

A) You may have to make do with what you have in the moment.

B) Spend your money where you know you will be accommodated.

Takeaway: It can be extremely frustrating when there are no accommodations for your disability. Unfortunately, there is no other choice but to accept the circumstances and make do with what you have in the moment. Generally, most businesses and people will try to accommodate your needs to the best of their abilities. However, if they cannot assist you, it may be better to spend your money elsewhere.

You are being harassed or hollered at by disrespectful men.
Consider the following,

A) A gentleman will not behave in a manner that would make a woman feel uncomfortable or sexualized.

B) You are not a piece of meat and should not allow any man to treat you in a disrespectful manner.

Takeaway: Oftentimes, women get harassed or hollered at by men in passing. Though a man may perceive that gesture as being a compliment to the woman, women view it differently. Making sly passes at a woman is not endearing nor is it attractive in any way. In fact, it is disrespectful and makes a woman feel uncomfortable, objectified and hyper-sexualized. A true gentleman will approach a woman cautiously and speak to her respectfully. If you are being harassed or hollered at by one man or a group of men, make sure to be aware of your surroundings and do your best not to pay too much attention to it.

Someone's child is being obnoxious or is out of control. Consider the following,

A) Some people do not discipline their children well enough.

B) Children can be temperamental.

Takeaway: It is a parent's responsibility to teach their children how to act appropriately and to discipline them accordingly. Children can be very temperamental, and some may not be as well-disciplined as other children. If you are out and about and someone's child is out of control or acting obnoxiously, exert self-control and either live with it or move elsewhere, should that be an option.

Someone is smoking cigarettes near you. Consider the following,

A) Second-hand smoke, in addition to first-hand smoke, can cause cancer.

B) Move somewhere else.

Takeaway: In the United States, an estimated 40 million adults smoke cigarettes and more than 16 million live with smoking-related diseases. Smoking cigarettes is a bad habit that is not conducive to the smoker or the people around them. First-hand and second-hand smoking can cause cancers in the body, accelerate aging by causing wrinkles in the skin, among other side effects like discoloring teeth. Not to mention that it smells bad. If someone is smoking near you, your best option is to move away. Cigarette smoking is the leading cause of preventable disease and death and with all the information available on the adverse effects of smoking, it is shocking that people continue to do it.

A woman is breastfeeding. Consider the following,

A) A baby's hunger has to be satisfied then and there.

B) Do not stare.

Takeaway: No mother looks forward to exposing herself in public, and sometimes there may not be any other place to do it. When babies are hungry, a mother's duty is to feed the baby and satisfy its hunger. This is especially true for mothers that have given birth recently, as newborns and young infants require immediate attention. Try to be understanding of the situation and do not stare.

A friend is acting drunk and disorderly. Consider the following,

A) A good friend will help the people they care about, even in situations that may cause embarrassment or muster up public dismay.

B) If your friend exhibits drunk and disorderly conduct often, then they have a substance abuse problem that requires professional help to overcome.

Takeaway: Sometimes people overdrink and surpass their personal limit of being in control. When this happens, a domino effect of other events often follows close behind. When a person is drunk, their ability to make sound decisions becomes extremely impaired. In fact, decisions made while drunk often lack thought and can cause emotional and physical damage, sometimes damage that is irreparable. If a friend is acting drunk and disorderly, then do your best to help them before their poor behavior gets them into trouble, or worse, gets you into trouble. If this behavior is typical of your friend, then do what you can to get them help and be mindful about being out with them in public, as behavioral patterns often get repeated.

Your patience is wearing thin. Consider the following,

A) Exhibit self-control.

B) Learn to practice patience.

Takeaway: Whatever the situation may be, there are many life moments that will test your patience. It is how we deal with these types of moments that make us stronger and more capable of overcoming other obstacles that may arise in the future. When your patience has worn thin, it is wise to exhibit self-control and learn to practice patience. These two characteristics are very important to cultivate if you want to lead a happy life.

A couple is displaying excessive affection for each other. Consider the following,

A) Love makes people act in ways they would not ordinarily.

B) Inappropriate behavior in public—affectionate or aggressive—is simply not acceptable.

Takeaway: When people are in love, in a new relationship or even drunk, they tend to express their feelings of happiness openly. Sometimes, couples can get caught up in the moment and may not realize they are creating a scene. If a couple is exhibiting inappropriate behavior in public, affectionate and/or aggressive, it is important to notify a public safety guard or even a police officer who can instruct the couple further. Please do not to engage in banter with them.

You got drunk and feel like you made a fool of yourself. Consider the following,

A) Many people have experienced or will experience an embarrassing drunken moment at some point.

B) Be mindful of your limits, especially when consuming alcohol.

Takeaway: We all need to let loose every now and then, and some people choose to do that by drinking alcohol. If you surpassed your personal limit, and feel like you made a fool of yourself, try not to be too hard on yourself. Everyone experiences an embarrassing moment at some point in their lifetime. However, every person has a limit, and it is important that if you decide to drink, to be responsible and a) know when to call it quits, and b) to arrange to be picked up and driven home.

You feel you were discriminated against. Consider the following,

A) If you have been discriminated against by an employee of an establishment you are visiting, then report your concerns to their boss.

B) Do not get drawn into back-and-forth banter with ignorant people.

Takeaway: The truth is, ignorance does exist and oftentimes it translates to discrimination. Being discriminated against, for any reason, can be an infuriating and/or demeaning experience. Firstly, no one goes about their day anticipating being discriminated against, and secondly, when it happens, it definitely is an experience that will catch anyone off their guard. If you have been discriminated against by an employee of an establishment you are visiting, then speak to their manager or write a letter to the CEO. If you are being discriminated against by a civilian or a group of ignorant people, aim to get yourself to a safe spot so that words do not escalate to violence.

You got arrested. Consider the following,

A) Every choice you make has a consequence.

B) Learn from the poor decisions you make in life.

Takeaway: There is nothing cool about getting arrested but it definitely is an opportunity to understand how it feels to have your rights and freedom stripped from you. Regardless of the circumstances surrounding your arrest—warranted or unwarranted—every choice you make has a consequence. Learn from all the decisions you make in life, especially the poor decisions, and be sure not to repeat them in the future.

RESOURCES

If you need help with:	Seek support from:	Call:	For more information, log onto:
Emergency	National Emergency Network	911	www.fcc.gov/consumers/guides/what-you-need-know-about-text-911
Suicide / Bullying / Counseling	National Suicide Prevention Lifeline	1-800-273-8255	www.suicidepreventionlifeline.org
Grief Support	Grief Share	1-800-395-5755	www.griefshare.org
Reporting Crimes	Crime Stoppers USA	1-800-222-8477	www.crimestoppersusa.org
Fertility	National Fertility Support Center	1-616-455-1499	www.fertilitysupportcenter.org
Domestic Violence	The National Domestic Violence Hotline	1-800-799-7233	www.thehotline.org
Child Abuse	National Child Abuse Hotline	1-800-422-4453	www.childhelp.org
Lesbian, Gay, Bisexual and Transgender Support	GLBT National Help Center	1-888-843-4564	www.glbthotline.org
Sexual Health	Planned Parenthood	1-877-686-5772 option #3	www.plannedparenthood.org
Disaster Relief	American Red Cross	1-800-733-2767	www.redcross.org
Youth Mentoring	Big Brothers Big Sisters of America	1-813-720-8778	www.bbbs.org
Detoxification / Rehabilitation	Substance Abuse and Mental Health Services Administration	1-800-662-4357	www.findtreatment.samhsa.gov
SAT / ACT Tutoring	Kaplan Test Prep	1-800-527-8378	www.kaptest.com/college-prep/getting-into-college/free-practice-test
Youth / Family Activities	YMCA USA	1-800-872-9622	www.ymca.net

If you need help with:	Seek support from:	Call:	For more information, log onto:
Sexual Assault	RAINN	1-800-656-4673	www.centers.rainn.org
Roadway Safety	National Highway Traffic Safety Administration	1-888-327-4236	www.nhtsa.gov
Airline Service Complaints and Comments	U.S. Department of Transportation	1-202-366-2220	www.transportation. gov/airconsumer/ file-consumer-complaint
End-of-Life Care Services	National Hospice and Palliative Care Organization	1-703-837-1500	www.nhpco.org
Addiction Recovery	Narcotics Anonymous	1-818-773-9999	www.na.org
Domestic Abuse	The National Domestic Violence Hotline	1-800-799-7233	www.thehotline.org

NOTES

Chapter 2

Mental Health Foundation. (2008) *Boiling Point: Problem anger and what we can do about it.* Retrieved from http://www.angermanage.co.uk/pdfs/boilingpoint.pdf.

Chapter 4

Vartanian, Oshin, Gorka Navarrete, Anjan Chatterjee, et al. (2013) *Impact of contour on aesthetic judgments and approach-avoidance decisions in architecture.* Proceedings of the National Academy of Sciences of the United States of America. 110(2):10446-10453. doi:10.1073/pnas.1301227110.

Chapter 5

ComPsych Corporation. (2013) *StressPulse Report.* Retrieved from http://visual.ly/compsych-stresspulse-survey.

The American Institute of Stress. (2001) *Workplace Stress.* Retrieved from https://www.stress.org/workplace-stress/.

Brummett, Beverly H., Michael A. Babyak, Rong Jiang, Svati H. Shah, Richard C. Becker, et al. (2013) *A Functional Polymorphism in the 5HTR2C Gene Associated with Stress Responses Also Predicts Incident Cardiovascular Events.* PLOS ONE. 8(12): e82781.

Gallup. (2017) *State of the American Workplace.* Retrieved from http://www.gallup.com/services/178514/state-american-workplace.aspx?g_source=EMPLOYEE_ENGAGEMENT&g_medium=topic&g_campaign=tiles.

Chapter 6

Lessne, Deborah, and Christina Yanez. (2016) *Student Reports of Bullying: Results From the 2015 School Crime Supplement to the National Crime Victimization Survey.* National Center for Education Statistics. NCES 2017015.

Kim, Young-Shin, and Bennett Leventhal. (2008) *Bullying and Suicide. A review.* International Journal of Adolescent Medicine and Health. 20(2), 133-154.

Chapter 7

Pickrell, Timothy M., Hongying R. Li, and Shova KC. (2016) *Traffic Safety Facts: Driver electronic device use in 2015.* National Highway Traffic Safety Administration. DOT HS 812 326.

Drews, Frank A., Monisha Pasupathi, and David L. Strayer. (2008) *Passenger and Cell Phone Conversations in Simulated Driving.* Journal of Experimental Psychology: Applied. 14(4), 392-400.

Strayer, David L., Frank A. Drews, and Dennis J. Crouch. (2016) *A Comparison of the Cell Phone Driver and the Drunk Driver.* Human Factors. 48(2), 381-391.

Chapter 8

Sanlorenzo, Martina, Mackenzie R. Wehner, Eleni Linos, John Kornak, et al. (2015) *The Risk of Melanoma in Airline Pilots and Cabin Crew - A Meta-analysis.* Journal of the American Medical Association—Dermatology. 151(1), 51-58. doi:10.1001/jamadermatol.2014.1077.

International Air Transportation Association. (2013) *New Year's Day 2014 marks 100 Years of Commercial Aviation.* Retrieved from http://www.iata.org/pressroom/pr/Pages/2013-12-30-01.aspx.

Chapter 9

American Foundation for Suicide Prevention. (2015) *Suicide Statistics.* Retrieved from https://afsp.org/about-suicide/suicide-statistics/.

National Center for Statistics and Analysis. (2014) *Traffic Safety Facts: Alcohol impaired driving: 2013 data.* National Highway Traffic Safety Administration. DOT HS 812 102.

USA Today. (2013) *Behind the Bloodshed: The Untold Story of America's Mass Killings.* Retrieved from http://www.gannett-cdn.com/GDContent/mass-killings/index.html#failures.

Mass Shooting Tracker. (2017) *U.S Mass Shootings, 2016.* Retrieved from https://www.massshootingtracker.org/data/2016.

Chapter 10

Chester, David S., and Nathan C. DeWall. (2017) *Combating the sting of rejection with the pleasure of revenge: A new look at how emotion shapes aggression.* Journal of Personality and Social Psychology. 112(3), 413-430. doi:10.1037/pspi0000080.

Hofmann, Wilhelm, Maike Luhmann, Rachel R. Fisher, Kathleen D. Vohs, and Roy F. Baumeister. (2014) *Yes, But Are They Happy? Effects of Trait Self-Control on Affective Well-Being and Life Satisfaction.* Journal of Personality. 82, 265-277. doi:10.1111/jopy.12050.

ABOUT THE AUTHOR

Avni Parekh is a highly driven, skilled public relations and strategic communications professional with a strong background in crisis communications and online reputation management, and has more than a decade of managerial, business development and marketing experience under her belt.

While writing *Be The Bigger Person: Scenarios & Solutions to Better Yourself,* Avni served as public relations manager at VITAS Healthcare, the nation's leading provider of end-of-life care. Based in their corporate headquarters for six years, Avni developed and executed all aspects of media outreach campaigns to increase exposure and support of local and national company initiatives with a high rate of success.

In addition to that, she created and implemented effective systems used to analyze various market trends. Her excellent written and verbal communication skills, coupled with her problem-solving abilities and genuine intention to help others was a perfect complement to effectively managing the company's online reputation for several years.

Prior to that, she served as director of operations at one of South Florida's premier yoga studios. Her strong interpersonal skills and ability to provide excellent customer service enabled her to successfully manage the studio's day-to-day operations while helping to steer its rapid financial growth.

A native of Miami, Avni earned a bachelor's degree in international relations from Florida International University.

To connect with her, visit www.AvniParekh.com.

92911138R00078

Made in the USA
Columbia, SC
02 April 2018